OUT AND ABOUT IN
QUEENSTOWN

FLORENCE PRESTON

A. H. & A. W. REED
WELLINGTON SYDNEY AUCKLAND

CONTENTS

The cover photograph is by K. & J. Bigwood

The back cover map is by Julius Petro

First published 1975

A.H. & A.W. REED LTD
182 Wakefield Street, Wellington
53 Myoora Road, Terrey Hills, Sydney 2084
11 Southampton Row, London, WC1B 5HA
also
16 Beresford Street, Auckland
165 Cashel Street, Christchurch

© 1975 Florence Preston

ISBN 0 589 00918 4

Set on IBM composer by A.H. & A.W. Reed Ltd
Printed by Dai Nippon Printing Company (Hong Kong) Ltd.

DEDICATION: For James

PREFACE

FOR those visitors not already acquainted with Queenstown this book may prove helpful as a guide to places of note within the town and the surrounding district.

For its early history I have relied chiefly upon Alfred Duncan's contemporary account *The Wakatipians*, and for legendary material I am deeply indebted to the late Herries Beattie, whose *Maori Lore of Lake, Alp and Fiord*, *The Maoris and Fiordland*, and *Our Southernmost Maoris* I bought and devoured in my youth as they came off the press.

For factual and biographical material in Chapters 5 and 10 I am grateful to the authors of the books acknowledged in the text.

For the rest I have relied on my own observations, conversations and experiences. The book makes no pretence at being either definitive or minutely accurate, and the wideawake will doutbtless find many more places, people and matters of interest as they move about the town and its environs or dip further into its short but exciting history.
Queenstown
1974   **F.P.**

THE AUTHOR: Florence Preston

"Before the town begins to stir, the magic will work for you."
National Publicity Studios

1

LONG TIME AGO

FULLY TO APPRECIATE any place of historic interest, one must first slide into the mood and time of its beginnings. In the stir and bustle of a modern tourist town this is not easy. To arrive in Queenstown in the evening when a dozen buses are spilling their weary contents on to the pavements, to pilot your car cautiously through the narrow congested streets, or to clump into a crowded camping ground with no thought in mind but to discard pack and boots, is certainly not the time for conjuring visions.

Nor are the places likely to be the milling streets at midday, the convivial bars of a later hour, nor even the beach strewn day-long with bodies browning in the sun.

But go in the early hours, perhaps to that same beach under the weeping willows at the near end of the bay, and before the town begins to stir the magic will work for you. . . .

It is a summer morning: no sound but the chorus of a million birds and the whisper of

mimic wavelets on the shore; nothing to see but silhouetted land-shapes like prehistoric monsters crowding down to the pale waters of the lake. The fancied sound of a snapping stick turns you half about. Smoke comes wavering from an out-door fire beside a bevy of *whares* (dwellings) on the end-shore. While women stoop over the earth-oven and children gather driftwood, tall brown men are beginning to look after the flax nets, there for birds, here for eels.

You have been seeing the *kaika* or small village of Tahuna, the Shallow Place, which existed until not very long before the first European settler came to this spot. The bay is shallow only by comparison; the lake that shelves quickly down to upwards of 30 metres, so clear that every stone can be seen on the bottom, is twenty times that in the deepest parts beyond this natural harbour.

The few hardy Maoris who lived this far south, moved on farther west when the first news of

These Maori villagers were painted by Lindauer in the 19th century, but in pre-Pakeha days the scene would have been much the same except for the European clothing. *Partridge Collection, Auckland City Art Gallery*

the arrival of the white strangers in their land was brought by nomad bands passing through to the greenstone coast. And so—if you're still oblivious to the present—the scene now changes. It is 1862, and in place of the Maori village is a single Pakeha hut belonging to Gilbert Rees, who has been granted a licence to run sheep on something like 202 000 hectares of the rough pasturage abounding in the valleys and gorges, on the hills and mountains that surround the great lake the Maori calls Whakatipua, the Hollow of the Giant.

There is a charming legend relating to this name—which lost a letter or two when the Pakeha took over. The villain of the tale was the giant Matau, so huge that when he was hungry he had only to step from one mountain top to the next and the next before reaching that spot on the coast where lived a tribe under the chieftainship of Tuwiriroa. There he would pick up a juicy morsel of maiden or child and carry her back to his inland den.

The time came when the victim was Manata, "as beautiful as a star", and the chief's own daughter. In his grief Tuwiriroa declared that whoever should recover his treasure might have her for wife. Then Matakouri, who had long loved Manata, though without hope because of his inferior rank, begged help of the tribal wizard in a daring bid to rescue the girl. There was a strong nor'wester whipping the coast, and having learned from the old wizard that the *tipua* (giant or demon) always fell asleep when this hot wind, the *mauru*, began to blow, he set off at speed over hill and vale, guided by the snores of the giant that shook the earth like thunder. He found his beloved still alive, and joyfully loosed her bonds. Then while the giant still slept he and Manata gathered great armfuls of fern and scrub, piled it close to the sleeper, and set it alight with Matakouri's firestick and tinder.

The giant groaned in his sleep, drew up his knees in pain, and awoke—too late. For months the great body went on burning, and so hot it became that the snows on the mountains all around began to melt until they ran in trickles, then streams, then torrents to fill the great hollow, shaped like a giant fifty miles long with his knees drawn up, that the fire had burned in the earth. And round about the new-formed lake, wherever the smoke had trailed, masses of small

Matakouri and Matau. *A.H. & A.W. Reed Collection*

grey bushes sprang up, ever after called *matakouri* (or *matagouri*) in honour of the brave youth who killed the wicked *tipua* and married the lovely daughter of the chief Tuwiriroa.

A more romantic explanation you'll surely agree, than the Pakeha theory of glacial action?

But it did not take Gilbert Rees long to discover that these thorny *matakouri* bushes were a menace to both man and beast. In fact he and his friend von Tunzelmann, who took up land on the western side of the lake, methodically set whole valleys alight on their initial exploration in search of country, so that in the following year when the first sheep arrived after their epic journey through the rocky wastes of Central Otago, the native pasture-grasses were in sole possession.

In the fair certainty of making a fortune on this country that he held in perpetual lease for a song, Gilbert Rees speedily erected two more clay-and-sapling buildings, helped by the three shepherds who had driven the flock. When the woolshed and the house were completed he scrambled over the trackless spurs and gullies round the lake, then through many miles of bush and swamp to bring home his wife, small daughter and newborn son, Cecil Walter,—the names that he passed on to those two high peaks on your left whose pinnacles are now all flushed with pink at the imminence of the sun, and

at anchor under the shelter of the park; large tourist launches at the piers; U-drive jets and humbler rowing boats drawn up on the shingle; and at the wharf the old *Earnslaw* is making steam, smoke pluming gaily from her slim red funnel. She has been mistress of the lake for the last sixty years, and is getting ready to carry you

Gilbert Rees's homestead at Kawarau Falls station, 1860s. *Lakes District Museum*

whose girdle of mist promises a perfect day.

At the raw little township of Invercargill in the far south, Rees bought an old whale boat and a pair of bullocks. He put the boat on sleds, loaded in a year's supplies, his family and a boat-hand and returned thus the 145 kilometres to the foot of the lake. There they yoked out the bullocks and added their weight to the cargo, then sailed the last 32 kilometres to the lonely spot where they proposed to make their home.

"Man proposes; God disposes." For two years only, the tiny community occupied the bay before their peace was shattered, their solitude violated.

And now, as if to emphasise the point, sound is impinging on your own dreaming solitude. Behind you in the town car engines are revving, milk bottles rattling, and an early bus is drawing in to the depot. With a jolt you come back from your contemplation of the past to see that the harbour, satin-smooth and shining now, is circled with craft: small launches, yachts and speedboats

to all sorts of interesting places during your stay.

As the sounds and activities of the day increase, especially those resulting from the present fever of expansion, it is not so difficult to imagine something of the ballyhoo that ensued when the goldrush broke out—to use a phrase of the time. And indeed it's an apt enough term for the fevers and the rash of diggings that followed upon the first discovery of gold in Otago. For nearly two years the multi-tude approached fitfully across the province, a fevered rush here, a pause for labour, another rush there, until it had almost reached the door-step of the quiet homestead at the bay.

The story has often been retailed from *The Wakatipians* by Alfred Duncan, one of the shep-herds who saw it all at first hand, but it is worth telling briefly again. It was early summer and shearing time, but at the scent of gold the shearers whom Rees had engaged had deserted almost to a man. It would be useless to try the Arrow 19 kilometres away, where all appeared

"The scent of gold." *Wilson & Horton*

night at the double task of mustering and shearing. It was the beginning of the greatest rush of all, and of the man who made the first discovery Duncan writes that he "made and kept the grip of probably more gold than any man who ever worked on the Shotover." Which is saying something, when you consider such recorded cases as the four claims that yielded 58 kilogrammes weight of gold in one day, or that of the two Maoris who gathered 11 kilogrammes in a single afternoon.

The diggers swarmed from end to end of the river and all its tributaries, often letting themselves down the stupendous rocky banks on ropes to pick, pan or cradle in what proved to be the richest river in the country—some say in the world.

Had it not been for the little homestead on the lake, many of these crazed treasure-seekers would have starved to death—as indeed some did, while it was no uncommon thing for men who had been lured too far into the completely unknown hinterland to return ravenous after not having eaten for days. Their only source of sustenance for many weeks was Gilbert Rees's sheep and the little tea and flour he could spare from the station supplies. These were soon exhausted, and although the whaleboat went off as often as

to be sharing in the spree, so Duncan took the boat on a recruiting expedition to the foot of the lake, then climbed over the Hector Range into the Nokomai Valley where, it was said, some of the diggers were out of luck. The rumour proved true, for the two men he persuaded to help with the shearing were so down and out that the one named Thomas Arthur refused to disembark at the homestead until Duncan provided him with a respectable pair of trousers in place of his own rags and tatters.

This was the man who upon the first Sunday thereafter took a walk with his mate to the river 5 kilometres distant, and returned at nightfall with a cupful of nuggets picked out of the crevices with a penknife.

"The men were completely off their heads," says Duncan. Nothing could hold them a moment longer at the station, and the few regulars remaining were obliged to toil day and

Gilbert Rees, 1827-98. The "father" of modern Queenstown. *Hocken Library*

Arthurs Point, Shotover, *circa* 1864. *Alexander Turnbull Library*

possible for replenishments, it could not always be back in time to save a desperate situation. Duncan tells of occasions when upon the arrival of the boat he would stand on the jetty in charge of a bag of flour, out of which he doled one pannikinful for each digger while Mr Rees stood guard with a loaded pistol "to prevent a rush". For his one cup of flour each digger paid half-a-crown (present-day equivalent, at least $2 NZ).

Although the pistol was never actually used, more than one troublemaker was knocked off the jetty to cool his passions in the lake. Gilbert Rees made a name for himself on the goldfields as an amateur pugilist, and his shepherds too had to be fighting fit to deal with those who found it more economical to find a sheep behind a boulder and slit its throat for themselves.

Few of the diggers carried guns, but there were plenty of fisticuffs and worse among these men of many nations who had come rushing over the

seas and from all parts of New Zealand to follow the gleam. All did not of course strike it lucky, and in the case of the penniless, Rees would never send a hungry man empty away. He also had a sense of humour, sufficient anyway to appreciate the reply of an Irishman whom he caught redhanded skinning a sheep. To the owner's irate query Paddy squared up to him and said, "I'll kill any bloody sheep that bites me!" Rees burst out laughing, and because the rascal was obviously starving, rode on and left him to his muttons.

Although he couldn't always return the compliment, the runholder himself was fully trusted by the diggers. Until the gold escort to and from Dunedin could extend its trips to this farthest outpost, the miners were happy to give their gold into Rees's keeping. The first yield of 25,000 ozs went down the lake in his station whaleboat.

9

Apparently few boggled at the high price of their monotonous diet. Killing and transport must of course have absorbed much of the profit, and the remainder was perhaps better in the run-holder's pocket than in the tills of the grog-shops that were the first amenities to appear in the impromptu canvas town.

For almost overnight there came into being a boom town of about six thousand souls, predominantly a floating population that came and went—came, to spend with incredible prodigality, and went out again to the wilds to earn replenishments. Grog-shops and shanties, hotels and hostelries, butchers and blacksmiths, ratting-pits, skittle-alleys, frame tents and sod huts, all crowded into the flat on the end-shore. Miners in buckskin trousers and heavy boots rode or plodded through the summer dust of the alley-ways, and every day or two there would lumber down the steeply curving track from above, a waggonload of welcome supplies. And welcome too, would be the sight of the randy little town to the weary bullocks and drivers who had struggled through dangerous rivers, over new-found passes and previously untrodden hills to deliver their loads of merchandise.

In a surprisingly short time, however, the scene changes: a first alpine winter has taught its bitter lesson, and before another year is out canvas has largely been replaced by more durable materials. A saw-pit has been established at the head of the lake, providing for sturdy all-purpose stores and several cottages. Even a few women other than camp followers are beginning to appear in this hitherto man's world. Civic buildings are under construction; the town boasts a council, a newspaper, a brass band, a police force. Gilbert Rees can put up his pistol now. More, he can find time to demolish his woolshed and to build in its place an hotel of brick and stone—one among scores less permanent.

A town is taking shape: early Queenstown with a cutter
at the wharf. *Lakes District Museum*

"The Eichardts of today is essentially the same building." *Lakes District Museum*

With a storey added by the German to whom he presently sold it, the Eichardt's of today is essentially the same building. See? Over there on the waterfront.

You're too hungry to want to see any more at the moment? Sorry to have kept you. . . . Yes, I do think bed-and-breakfast accommodation a good idea. It leaves you free to roam during the day, then at night it's fun trying out all the different dining places. . . . Yes, I suppose we have sampled nearly all of them. Most, including the hotels, are much of a muchness: expensive Continental meals with a few special New Zealand dishes, gay interiors, sometimes astonishing views, and so many of them accompanied by the din that passes nowadays for music. Quite literally, you can't hear yourself nor anyone else speak. If they just wouldn't use those amplifiers! "Orgyfiers", James calls them since a youthful caller assured us that there was something Wildly Exciting in the way these bands worked gradually up from a quiet throbbing to a tremendous and sustained burst of sound.

Out of respect for their eardrums and a desire to enjoy their table conversation, we usually take guests now to the Country Lodge, an attractive hotel on Fern Hill. Quiet harmonious decor, soft concealed lights *and* soft concealed music, excellent food and service—oh dear, now I've made you hungrier than ever. . . .

Yes, certainly; I'll be very happy to show you something of the town after breakfast . . . Right? The far end of the Mall then, at ten.

"The citizens keep a jealous eye on any infringement" of the natural beauty of their town.
National Publicity Studios

2

TOWN AND AROUND

FOR the first day or two after their arrival in Queenstown most people find this high dry atmosphere a little enervating. Although there's much to see and do beyond it, lassitude may tempt you to devote this period to exploring the town itself.

I still stumble over that word "town". Those of us who knew Queenstown when it was only a village of less than 900 souls still find it difficult to adjust to the new status it has so rapidly acquired. Indeed, were it not for the fact that its population is every bit as fluctuating as in its rakish infancy, it might appear to be on its way to becoming a city. It's certainly on the move; wherever you look round the circling hills, a half-finished or just-completed building catches the eye; and even on the flat, where all available space was taken up a hundred years ago, enlargement is rapidly being accomplished by bulldozers biting into the hills. Although its permanent residents currently number just over 2000, on an average the daily floating population is ten times that, with ever-rising tendencies.

The question of how to cope with this swift expansion and yet retain something of the town's unique charm is not being wholly neglected. The citizens themselves keep a jealous eye on any infringement of its own townplanning edicts that the Borough Council might be prepared to countenance, as witness the battle long fought and recently won by the local "guardians" concerning the proposed building of a high-rise hotel on reserve land, a proposal unacceptable on both counts, but to which both Council and Government had given their sanction.

I was only a teenager—the most impressionable of ages—when I first saw the village. I often wish I could see and *feel* it again for the first time. But ecstasy is seldom repeated in the same context. You go on enjoying the light and shade on the Remarkable Mountains, the amazing sunsets over Mt Nicholas, the dreaming lake—or the angry sea that in a different mood it can readily become; but the wine of the gods you once drank in blissful draughts has become through familiarity just good fresh mountain air, and all the wooded seclusions that made you feel like the Girl of the Limberlost or David Livingstone are now cleared away and built over. . . . But enough; it wasn't the past we set out to explore, only the town of today.

The Mall is an obvious place to begin. Every time I see this resurrected waterwheel at the entry I have a frustrating urge to give it an almighty push. Although an interesting relic of the days when running water was used as the driving power for the stampers that crushed the goldbearing quartz, it does have the unhappy effect of cluttering the view that formerly introduced you to the village as you rounded the library corner into the narrow main street, with glory at its end.

Still, the Mall itself is a blessing. Here you may wander at will without fear of stepping under wheels, and do your shopping in peace. Or you may watch the world go by in a kaleidoscope of colour and an astonishing variety of dress or undress, while sipping the drink of your choice at a pavement cafe in true Continental style.

Several of the shops in the Mall are of gold-era origin, some, behind their modern facades, being solid structures of stone. A happy tendency towards building again in the local stone and timbers, coupled with a new consciousness of harmony in design, is evident in some of the more recent buildings.

The Trading Post, reconstructed within the shell of the old Embassy Theatre, is an example of what imaginative design coupled with a feeling for the past can accomplish. ("Shell" perhaps conveys the wrong impression; the facade of this building is one metre thick, of eight or nine brick courses, whitewashed outside and as solid, not surprisingly, as on the day when the last brick was laid.) From a varied collection of Victoriana in the shape of windows, doors, iron grilles and so on, the builders have constructed a series of small shops on different floor levels, each attractive in its individual way.

Though the wheel is an interesting reminder of the past, it "clutters the view" down the pedestrian mall, Ballarat Street. *National Publicity Studios*

The balcony facing into the Mall is particularly so. And an unusual feature is that the roof to the whole can be opened and closed in accordance with the weather.

Inevitably, gift shops have moved into town with the tourist. We think—and I believe without prejudice—that these shops can at least hold their own with any of their equivalents we've seen overseas. While most have a wide variety of distinctively New Zealand gifts, this boutique in the Arcade is even more localised in its appeal. Its stocks consist entirely of goods manufactured from merino wool and skins. (The hardy, soft-woolled Merino sheep was introduced from Austria in 1859, and has largely stocked the mountain runs of the Wakatipu ever since.) You've never passed your money over a counter like that before? It's a woolpack, such as the farmer sends his clip in to the sales.

But enough of shops and shopping. The Mall is also used as a kind of outdoor community centre. Here you might happen upon the easels or the booths of some local art exhibition or a flower show. And in the evenings during the peak holiday period you may like to watch the kind of youthful high jinks from which the older generation usually prefer to absent themselves.

Should the weather prove unseasonable such functions, together with nightly dancing, are held in the Centennial Hall, there above the Sports Ground. The Hall is also used as a fairground or fun-park during the Christmas-New Year week.

Here, just across from the waterwheel, is where you'll collect your mail. No, the Post Office is of comparatively recent vintage, as you can see by the perpendicular setting of the stone, but there, just over the old stone bridge beside it, is a group of buildings that really do belong to the past. The old library—as distinct from the equally attractive new one—the Borough Council rooms, and the County Council offices opposite, have all pased their century mark, and the gigantic sequoia trees in the immediate vicinity reached theirs in 1973. They are known as justice trees, and the seat around the one outside the courtroom was placed there for your comfort, that you might sit at ease in its shade while waiting for your case to come on. At least, that was the reason for their planting at a time when the court was kept very busy indeed, even without the help of traffic offences.

The perfect masonry of these old buildings was the work of the mason who also built for himself the stone cottage in which we lived during the war while waiting for James to return. Just round this corner and opposite the car park you'll see it, a few doors from the Anglican church—the one with the lychgate. Much newer is the church above it, also built in local stone, and also attractive in its way.

We hadn't meant to live right in the village— and thereby hangs a tale, too long to tell here in detail. Sufficient that when James came on leave to see the property he had agreed to buy on nothing but my burning recommendation, he reneged on the deal, declaring the house too decrepit and too isolated for us to live in during his absence. Anyway, it is now built over with scores of holiday houses, and we shouldn't have cared for that. So instead of buying an old stone house and barn on the Frankton arm of the lake, with a private boat harbour, 2.8 gorsey hectares and wonderful possibilities for a garden, we rented this prim little cottage down here near the waterfront.

Although there was wailing and gnashing of teeth among the family, the cottage did have the advantage of being handy to the park, which was almost as unvarying a delight as the lake.

Time has brought changes here too. This long spit of land enclosing the harbour on the south was originally quite bare except for the ubiquitous matakouri and a vanished *pa* (village), Te Karoro—doubtless named after the gulls whose descendants still keen in the bay though the sea coast is 48 kilometres away. The spit was not made use of during the rush; but when first the

"The perfect masonry of the old buildings." The old Anglican church, Queenstown. *J.T. Salmon*

The lake has its stormy moments—but even these have their own beauty. *Lakes District Museum*

15

"The park, almost as unvarying a delight as the lake."
National Publicity Studios

alluvial gold yields, then those from the more difficult dredging and quartzmining, became seriously diminished well before the end of the century, the Government turned its attention to keeping the rapidly declining town alive by helping the citizens to develop both its tourist potential and the land round about.

Except for the non-bearing Peninsula run, the licence to Gilbert Rees's enormous holding had been cancelled early in 1863. The area was declared a goldfield, and a dozen years later settlement was encouraged by the survey of the land into smaller free-holdings. With a farming population to back its economy and a unique beauty that was already attracting tourists, the Government decided to enhance that attraction by planting here what they called the Domain.

The result of their forethought was the park we knew in our youth. Its forest of pines, in whose depths you could count the world for lost, has since been drastically thinned, but splendid specimen trees both deciduous and evergreen still line the walks—beech, ash, cedar of Lebanon, and the huge scarlet oaks near the gate, which I hope you'll come to see when they are all afire in the autumn.

From time to time many trees were removed too, to make room for the bowling green and tennis courts, and more recently for the skating rink. You will not need to wait until the depth of winter to use the rink, but winter skating was all we knew until six or seven years ago. This long pond with the humpback bridge was our stamping ground. Except at weekends, when everyone came, it was appropriated in the early afternoons by the housewives, joined later by schoolchildren and later still by the men.

As newcomers, small son and daughter learned the art speedily and with ease, but my own protracted novitiate afforded the onlookers much merriment and myself much pain. Nonetheless, some of my warmest memories hover round that hard-frozen pond, which now you see starred with summer waterlilies.

Queenstown is at its most beautiful in winter. Although the nights are frigid, the brief days are bright with sunshine and free of wind—unless you live in the gorge!—that sometimes plagues us in summer. Ski boots ring hard on the frozen roads, and under shaded banks icicles hang like chandeliers. Sunset colours stain the white mountain tops and find reflection in the lake, whose summer turquoise and blues nave given place to deepest jade.

Although it is always sad to see a tree felled, one good thing about the more judicious thinning of this north side of the park is that now you can enjoy an unimpeded view of the whole western terrace and its backgrounds. On the far left, two of the newest subdivisions lie half revealed among trees on the foothills of Ben Lomond. The farthest, Sunshine Bay, is my own favourite of all the outer suburbs, because the promoters have had the wisdom to leave the native cover as intact as possible, so that each house nestles in its own pocket of bush.

Before a series of fires in our own time destroyed most of it, all the slopes on the north side of the lake were covered with either beech forest or mixed bush, which explains why an operatic chorus of birdsong greeted those who first came this way. The morons who had the dim idea of introducing the lesser ermines to counteract the also-introduced rabbit, were responsible for its drastic diminishment. But when you go one day into the back country you will, I hope, experience at least some pale echo of that former delight.

The houses at Sunshine Bay are for the most part in pleasing congruity with their backgrounds. Apropos, I recall how a much-travelled stranger, unable to retain a former aloofness as our bus approached Queenstown, said aloud in amazement, "But this beats anything in the world—even Switzerland!"

So James and I went to Switzerland to see if we agreed. We had a base at Montreux, near the east end of Lake Geneva. The view from our balcony was astonishingly like that from our own western terrace, especially the mountain that was so like Cecil Peak. But, unlike our own, the waters of the Swiss lake were murky. This does not mean however that we were not entranced with Switzerland, nor that we agreed with the stranger in the bus. What makes it to our minds a more beautiful country than our own, is what you might call the human touch: men have built there for centuries and always with an eye to harmony, so that their lovely steep-roofed houses do not affront but enhance the landscape.

Looking across from the park however, you

"Ask for a window table...." *National Publicity Studios*

may note that New Zealanders are at last beginning to develop an aesthetic sense in this respect; at least some of our designers are taking to heart the prime precept that buildings must be in harmony with their natural backgrounds. And although there are still pockets of ugliness to be cleared away—and not just in buildings!—the idea is making headway.

Although riven with gullies, that wooded gap separating Sunshine Bay and Fern Hill from the town proper may sooner or later be built upon, but happily not yet. After a pleasant suburb of largely permanent homes, the hotels, hostels, motels and houses begin to jostle for place on the steep hillsides below the Borough camping ground and above the One-Mile—a name loosely employed to cover the street, the tree-lined promenade, and the stream at which both have their ending.

All the streams flowing into the lake on the eastern side proved auriferous, and the miners named them thus prosaically, as for instance the

Two-Mile, the Five-Mile and so on. Except for the Bucklerburn at the head of the lake, most have retained these odd names.

And so the panorama continues until you come to that straight gash in the pinewoods on Cemetery Hill, where brightly-coloured beetles appear to be climbing slowly up the wall and coming as slowly down. At the chalet on the top, each disappears at regular intervals into the hill, reappearing shortly to join those descending.

You've been asked to lunch at the chalet with a friend? Well, on your way to the depot slip in to see the little cemetery on your left; there are some interesting gravestones, many in languages you'll perhaps not be able to read, but they tell a story just the same. And if you're interested in vintage cars, there's an excellent collection in a new building on the right.

Safe? You mean the gondola lift? Oh yes, very safe. A freak accident, resulting in the deaths of two passengers, did happen in December 1974 but the operators are confident such a thing will never happen again. An inspector is permanently employed and the machinery is checked over daily. But if you're inclined to be squeamish I'd advise sitting in the gondola with your back to the hill, otherwise you may have the constant feeling that you're about to bump into it. And when you go to look out on top, be sure not to stand too close to the edge lest you be bowled over by the stunning view. Ask for a window table, too. It's worth an extra dollar, but you can have it for free.

A touch of Switzerland. Lower terminal of the gondolas that lift you to an unforgettable alpine view. *National Publicity Studios*

Above: "Splendid specimen trees line the walks." *National Publicity Studios*

Below: The gentlest, friendliest of outdoor games, played in an idyllic setting.
National Publicity Studios

3

NOT FAR AFIELD

I'M OFTEN ASKED by people visiting Queenstown for only a day or two, how they should best employ their limited time. Not only to these but also to those ready for a day's relaxation between scheduled excursions my advice is: Why not just have a day of pottering in the immediate vicinity of the lake itself? After all, isn't this primarily what you came to see?

A walk in the park is not to be scorned. You'll have seen larger and more magnificent parks, possibly even more charming ones, but seldom one affording more magnificent views.

Or you may like to rest awhile in the shade of the weeping willows on the end-shore, or join those bodies baking in the sun a little closer to the tiny waves that endlessly *spt-spt* upon the shingle. In midsummer heat you might suddenly be moved to cool off, but the temperature of the

glacier-fed water that shelves so quickly to overhead depths comes as something of a shock, and it won't be long before you're stretched again on sun-warmed terra firma.

In our youth we always swam here in the summer—there were dressing sheds and even a divingboard. But nowadays swimmers usually go to the school baths, open to the public in holiday times. Some of the hotels, too, have their own swimming baths.

If you prefer solitude to the crowd that is almost certain to be on the end-shore, cross the stream just beyond the children's playground and turn up the south shore of the bay.

Here under the shelter of the park there's a succession of small secluded beaches, partitioned as it were by here a large rock, there a tree trunk yearning towards the water; and for a short

"Bodies baking in the sun." But there are great trees for cool shade, and the glacier-fed waters are bracingly refreshing. *National Publicity Studios*

Above: In the 1860s, water was not a tourist amenity but the lifeblood of the sluice mines, of which this Shotover plant was one example. *Auckland Star Collection, Alexander Turnbull Library*

Opposite: Golden Terrace. It could be one of the mining villages in its heyday — except for the great exotic trees, which would have been mere saplings 100 years ago. *National Publicity Studios*

distance offshore the lake is shallower, therefore warmer, than at the main beach. These make happy pottering-places for children, and the kowhai trees provide shade for those whose aim is merely peaceful observation. An eye must be kept on small bathers however; just beyond their depth, several privately-owned launches, perhaps a yacht or two, are temptingly moored.

Depending upon the time of day, there will be various sights and activities across the bay to interest the watchfully idle. With luck, you may see the amphibian come winging in, to land with a gentle swish on the water. It may have come to take a party of trampers into one of the Fiordland sounds, or some fishermen perhaps, to try their luck with the fly in one of the renowned but remote lakes or rivers in the Hollyford area.

A few of those sputtering little U-drive speedboats are almost certain to be in action, or a jetboat may go roaring out of sight and sound, its occupants fitted with bright orange lifejackets. For the bay itself is far from shallow, and beyond

it the depth of the lake varies from roughly 275-400 metres. Even in summer the water temperature never rises above 52°F (11°C), and in such conditions an untoward accident could have fatal results.

At 1.30 pm the steamer *Earnslaw* will come sweeping round the bay on her return from the luncheon cruise in the Frankton Arm. And round about 2 pm—repeating their 9 am schedules—the service boats that have been stationed in a colourful line at the jetties and wharfs begin to fill with trippers bound for one or another of various excursions. But when they've gone chugging out of sight beyond the harbour, you'll probably turn lazily over and think how delicious it is to have absolutely nothing to do, nowhere to go. . . .

To most of us however, there usually comes a time when idleness begins to pall. What else is there to see and do in the immediate environs? Well, if you feel in need of a little exercise after that laze in the sun, it's only a half-hour walk along the Frankton road to the Golden Terrace Mining Town. . . . No, not strictly a ghost-town, but certainly a very convincing replica. If you picture it multiplied in size by several streets you'll get quite an accurate idea of what Queenstown looked like in its mining heyday. Except for the variety of attire that has long since succeeded the obligatory crinoline and moleskins, the all-nations crowd that is almost certain to be milling around here today is at least faintly reminiscent of those stirring times when bearded Britons and their women mingled in the town with pigtailed Chinese and seasoned diggers fresh from the Californian and Australian goldfields. And it requires only a small effort of the imagination to see the gold escort, drawn by four matching bays and accompanied by armed red-coat outriders, dashing up to the door of the bank, to have transferred into its strongboxes the weekly bullion that will eventually be shipped to London.

Rex and Trevor Woodbury, the two brothers who planned and constructed this replica of a goldmining town on the evidence of old photo-graphs and documents, have even used on the shop fronts and business premises the local pioneer names appropriate to each. The extra-ordinary thing is that although, with the exception of the school, all are quite new, you can easily mistake them for century-old buildings. This effect has been achieved by the use of a dull greyish timber stain, but even more convincingly by genuine fittings such as doors and window-frames, skirtings, doorsteps, dadoes and adver-tising signs that have been retrieved from old buildings during demolition operations in the district.

The interiors are furnished with literally thousands of authentic pieces, many donated by descendants of the early inhabitants, others bought at far and near clearing sales by the promoters of this fascinating project.

The premises include a general store, a hair-dresser-and-tobacconist's shop, a bookseller-and-stationer's, a confectioner's, a wine-and-spirit merchant's, a timber merchant's, a smithy, livery-and-bait stables, the *Wakatip Mail* office and printing room, the Antrim Arms hotel, the

Sutherland's smithy, Golden Terrace. The old blacksmiths were engineers as well as farriers; they made and mended the mining machinery. *National Publicity Studios*

visitors' lounge—of the Antrim Arms, with its genuine gold-leaf window signs, immense stone fireplace, smoked beams, and seats inviting relaxation after the stress of absorbing with wonder that feast of antiques chosen and arranged with such vivid imagination and consummate skill.

The village is charmingly set amidst pines, bluegums and green hillocks on an 8 hectare site, over which you may wander at will, and through which runs a small stream furnished with a natural waterfall. These last will be as useful as they are ornamental, for the activity that brought such villages into existence has not been lost sight of; it is planned to establish by the stream a full-sized waterwheel and batteries for demonstrating the old quartz-crushing operations.

Such abandoned mining equipment should not be too difficult to procure; examples are still to

Bank of New Zealand and, least dispensible of all, Her Majesty's gaol. They are arranged on either side of a narrow thoroughfare complete with period vehicles, pump and water-trough, tethering rings and hitching-posts, and there's a picket-fenced cottage on a rise at the head of the street.

Each interior merits prolonged inspection, but some of us will be detained longest by the wealth of treasures and lifelike models in the cottage; some by the massive forge, huge bellows, smelter, tongs and other iron accessories in the smithy; while horse-lovers will delight in the cobbled stables with their stalls and feeding troughs, looseboxes, driving harness and riding equipment. (By some miracle this new-old building even *smells* like a stable.) But I shouldn't be surprised if you settle in the end for the saloon—now a

A contemporary artist's view of the Phoenix mine at Skippers, 1887. *Pascoe Collection, Alexander Turnbull Library*

be found in various remote parts of Central Otago. I myself once happened upon a wheel and stampers, still in good condition, standing gaunt and incongruous in a vast area of unhabited tussock country at the back of the Raggedy Range.

Meantime, in the office of the Golden Terrace Mining Company, a model of an ore-crushing battery, set in a beautifully-designed miniature of the Shotover district, is constantly at work. And on the same display table are shown also the various methods that were used in the recovery of alluvial gold: panning, cradling, sluicing, and dredging.

I hope you won't miss seeing for yourself this wonderfully evocative replica of a goldmining village, of which I've given the merest sketch. If you don't care for walking or haven't your own car, a coach leaving Queenstown at 9.15 am will take you there on the return drive from Deer Park Heights—the other part of a double excursion to these two places of unusual interest on either side of the Frankton Arm.

Queenstown Airport beckons the visitor arriving by air. The departing guest looks wistfully back at it as his aircraft heads for home. *National Publicity Studios*

Above: The Kawarau bridge today. Downstream there must be a fabulous amount of gold that this dam/bridge failed to uncover. *A.H. & A.W. Reed Collection*

Below: Golf demands concentration, but at the 19th the players will look up at the Remarkables. *National Publicity Studios*

4

THE FRANKTON ARM

SHOULD YOU HAVE your own or a hired car, a fuller and even more rewarding drive than the coach trip can be taken round the Frankton Arm. (In this case you'll need first to call at one or another of the Queenstown bureaux for the dollar token which will admit your car to the deer park.)

When telling children the legend of the lake I always represent this small protruberance as a wart on the giant's knee. In reality Wakatipu's one-only arm, tiny by comparison with the main body, is about 6 x 1.5 kilometres. Especially at the far end, where it lingers on the beaches before gathering to its exit in the Kawarau River, the water is quite shallow, comparatively warm, and perfectly safe for bathing. Which probably explains why, apart from the view of the middle reach of the lake and those spectacular sunsets over Mt Nicholas, so many have chosen to build holiday houses on the terraces at Frankton.

On the flat land opposite, the Wakatipu Golf Course lies plainly open to view. But you might spare a minute—supposing you didn't arrive by air—to slip through the gates to the more secluded Queenstown airport, if only to see the glorious setting of the handsome new terminal that has recently replaced the old: hills to the left, mountains to the right, and the runways merging gradually into the green waves of the Kawarau Valley and the gentle hills of the Arrow Downs.

In this age of air travel the Frankton flats have proved a boon to close-confined Queenstown; and those houses massed like seabirds on a sanctuary speak the popularity of the terraces. But for a hundred years before the present development Frankton was only a very small settlement, even though in the beginning the authorities favoured building the main town in this more open and accessible spot. Not surprisingly however, business promptly followed where the miners themselves had congregated—close to the initial source of supply at the homestead on Queenstown Bay.

Originally part of the Peninsula run on which Gilbert Rees settled when the remainder of his holding was declared a goldfield, the small settlement was named after his wife Frances. There remain of early Frankton only the County Hospital—soon to be abandoned in favour of a site in Queenstown—a substantial old home almost hidden in trees, the ruins of a flourmill on this side of the bridge, and the Peninsula homestead, now a motor camp, down there among the willows on the other.

There was of course no bridge in those early days. Access to the peninsula was by punt—right up until 1926. The bridge then built was both a costly and an unusual piece of engineering, undertaken by the Kawarau Mining Company. Not that the company required a bridge, but the Government of the day, with some thought in mind of opening a route to the south, would agree to the building of a dam at the lake's outlet only on condition that a traffic-way be built upon the same foundations and at the company's expense.

"Photographs of this bridge in the building are to be seen in various museums." This one is from the Lakes District Museum at Arrowtown.

At a time when the goldmining industry had long been languishing, the promotion of this company caused no small stir, not only in New Zealand but also in England and Australia. No one doubted that quantities of gold still lay in the Kawarau-Clutha system of rivers; of necessity it had previously been harvested mainly on the banks and beaches. If the lake could be dammed at its outlet at the Kawarau falls, then the bed would be fully exposed in the upper reaches, and partly in the lower all the way to the sea. So long as the work was done while the snows feeding the lake were winter-bound, there would be little danger of its rising beyond control.

The prospectus for this bold scheme duly came out, capital came pouring in, shares changed hands at fantastic prices, speculators and sub-companies bought claims blind, and miners were engaged to work them. The parent company blasted away most of the rocky falls, built their dam and bridge, and issued a general invitation to the grand opening ceremony—or more properly, the closing ceremony.

Photographs of this bridge in the building are to be seen in various museums, but I prefer to picture the scene on the occasion when at last the tapes were cut and the sluicegates lowered. The gala day dawned, and crowds from far and near came to witness the miracle that would realise all their private dreams. From boat and car and buggy they came streaming down to the bridge where as yet the waters of the lake hurried white and foaming over the humbled falls into the deeps of the glass-green river. But in moments all that energy was to be bridled, and then . . .

The ministers of Mines and Public Works, the local mayor and councillors, the managing directors and chief engineers assembled on the dais, and the usual congratulatory speeches were followed by the official opening of the bridge.

And now came the great moment. To the accompanying rattle and grind of hawsers, weights and winches, the ten sluicegates of the dam were slowly lowered.

Naturally there was something of a tidal wave on the Frankton beaches, but wet knees and the frightened screams of children were a trifling price to pay for the knowledge that the gates had indeed called halt to those billions of gallons of water. Hardly a trickle seeped through the barricade, and soon the river-level was perceptibly falling.

It was a long time before the excitement of the crowd began to cool a little, before doubt crept in, to be succeeded by horror, anger, despair. The muddied water lay now stationary, no longer a river, but a wide lagoon.

The rumour spread that better results would be seen below the mouth of the Shotover, but when those vitally concerned hurried down to the junction, the cause of the fiasco was plainly evident. Blithely the waters of the Shotover were still careering down the Kawarau bed—except for that part of the volume which had flowed quietly backward to find its own level in the trough between the junction and the bridge. Incredible as it may seem to us in hindsight, no one seems to have thought of also damming the tributary Shotover.

Had this been the only snag it might yet have been overcome, but other difficulties were soon exposed. Tailings and old mining debris had so filled the bed that little new ground was laid bare; also, from bank to bank almost all the way down both the Kawarau and the Clutha into which it flows, a series of unsuspected rock bars acted as locks for pools too deep to work.

Inevitably the following days witnessed a panic reaction, with closing of bank doors, insolvencies, abscondings, and tears. And not surprisingly, an attempt of the parent company to raise fresh capital for damming the Shotover and the Arrow was a complete failure.

What so many lost on the swings however, the Wakatipu district gained on the roundabouts. That immovable bridge served as inspiration to the Roads Board to venture on what many had thought the impossible task of opening a road to the south, round the foothills of the Remarkables. And the bitter economic depression of the early 1930s provided the labour.

Working entirely without the aid of machinery, with nothing but gelignite for blasting and the picks and shovels in their hands, men from all walks of life—at ten shillings a week!—carved this twisting 48 kilometre road from the mountain side in something under ten years. The result of their labours, opened in 1936, was a one-way gravelled road with passing bays—now a paved two-lane highway.

"The Highland stags of Otago" is how wildlife historian Bruce Banwell described these descendants of wild Scottish ancestors. Here in the Deer Park they are shot by cameras, not by bullets.
National Publicity Studios

Look back a moment after crossing the bridge and you'll see the ten sluicegates, open now, but otherwise just as they were seen by the excited crowd on that fateful day half a century ago.

Shortly after crossing the bridge you turn right onto the Peninsula, part of which has of recent years been developed as an area for more holiday homes. But above this fringe the hilly remainder is still the domain of animals: unusual animals to find so close to civilisation, and I think you'll find your dollar toll well spent on seeing them.

Here's the tollgate on the left, about halfway along the main Peninsula road. The privately-owned road winds in easy gradations to nearly 900 metres above sea level, and as well as enjoying stunning views in all directions from the top, you'll be delighted to see on the way, wandering freely on virgin tussock country, herds of many-coloured goats and various kinds of deer. Most of the latter are the common red deer, but there are a few fallow deer and chamois, and a recent proud addition is a wapiti stag—our name for the American elk. He was an expensive luxury at $800, and the mate is is hoped to secure for him will be even more costly.

You're quite likely to mistake the little chamois, with his single pair of horns, for one of the goats; on the other hand, the large shaggy-haired Tibetan thar looks much more like a deer than the goat he really is. Be sure to bring your camera. In particular there are wonderful shots to be taken of goats and kids pausing in their play on the natural rocky outcrops to stare at the passing car.

The October-November period is not the best of times to visit the deer park; most of the animals are looking rather draggled while shedding their winter coats, and the stags are still in the velvet, so somewhat shy. But by December they'll face the camera proudly, dis-

Beach below Kelvin Heights. "It will be a great day for the elderly when someone discovers how to silence a speedboat" – but the youngsters revel in the excitement. *National Publicity Studios*

playing to all comers their splendid new antlers.

Driving on beyond the tollgate along the Peninsula road, you pass through an interesting new development variously known as Kelvin Heights or the Alpine Village. Its curving streets are attractively laid out, all wiring is confined underground, and house plans, while individual and various, must conform to certain aesthetic and practical standards.

Just below Kelvin Heights and at the end of both the Frankton Arm and the road is what we think the best of the Queenstown beaches. Although you've had to drive right round the Arm to reach it, the time is foreseeable when a bridge or causeway will connect Queenstown with this end of the Peninsula, which here shelves narrowly into the main lake right opposite the town.

This tongue of land behind our favoured picnicking spot is furred all over with pines and rowan trees—or was. The plantations are now being partially removed in the making of what one of its architects, who has designed many such courses overseas, declares will be an international golf course second to none. Shelter for the beach however, will remain. You'll still be able to park against a tree trunk to watch the skiers skimming the waters of the Arm, which by common consent seems to be the arena for this exciting but noisy summer sport.

It will be a great day for the elderly when someone discovers how to silence a speedboat. But the young apparently enjoy this cacophonous means of transport; and when Son One brings his *Zip* to the lake we sometimes even join the merry gang ourselves to watch the family skiing. The launching jetty for speedboats is close to the main wharf in Queenstown, and it takes about ten minutes to convey us to this uncrowded beach. But don't regret having come the long way round; otherwise you wouldn't have seen—well, all that you've seen on the way.

5

BY LAUNCH TO CECIL PEAK

BE SURE to wear an extra woolly or, better, a removable jacket or windbreaker. On even the hottest day it can be nippy on the lake in a speeding launch, yet when you get in among the hills of the Cecil Peak station you may meet with torrid temperatures.

Beyond the harbour the south arm of the lake opens to view, and you can see the road to Kingston weaving round the foothills of the Remarkables. The mountains themselves require no introduction; you've seen them rearing their triple cone to nearly 2400 metres from almost every part of Queenstown.

It is a brief trip. Once round the harbour buoys, *Viking* heads directly across to Cecil Peak, the nearer of the two mountains dominating the far side of the lake. As you come into the bay, past the small bluegum island that from Queenstown looks so exactly like a tall-masted ship, the launch reduces speed. And now, all passion spent, she is riding smoothly on the bottle-green waters whose depth you can sense even if you don't already know that the bed of the lake lies 180 metres below.

Still in deep water, *Viking* draws into the landing. Passengers are collecting their

Cecil Peak sheep station, where visitors see something of high-country farming methods. *O. Petersen*

belongings, or exclaiming in a variety of tongues over the height and spread of the gumtrees and the cliffs that rise abruptly behind them.

Your host is waiting on the wharf with a helping hand or a word of welcome. The sight of so many visitors crossing the plank doesn't disturb him in the least; he's used to it. For twice every day some scores of tourists take this unique opportunity of seeing at first hand something of the way of life enjoyed or endured on the high-country runs in the Wakatipu basin. (On this particular run, all is cheerfully endured that

can't be cured and the remainder is enjoyed to the hilt.)

Round the lake there are some eight of these stations, though needless to say they don't all open their homes to visitors on the grand scale. Such hospitality is surely exceptional anywhere—but then, the Lucases are exceptional people.

Other members of the family you will meet presently, but you will already have noted that your host is a friendly person, and the twinkle in his eye leads you to guess that his attitude to life is no dour one. In fact, Popeye Lucas has tremen-

Host "Popeye" Lucas helps a visitor ashore at Cecil Peak. *National Publicity Studios*

dous personality. In age and appearance—no, his eyes don't pop—he is not unlike his chinny namesake of the cartoon-strip, though it is extremely doubtful if the Sailor Man's exploits could hold a candle to those that have made the name of Popeye Lucas almost a legend in his time.

His deeds of daring as a bomber pilot in one of the New Zealand squadrons of the RAF during the Second World War won him a universal reputation as well as a DFC and bar.

After the war, the courage and determination, the spirit and resource that had carried him through the gruelling years that he yet makes so light of, swept him on to an equally noteworthy record in the civilian world he returned to.

Not surprisingly, the miles—and I refuse to translate this into kilometres!—of red tape he became entangled in while trying to persuade the Government to license private enterprise in commercial and tourist aviation, did not deter him. With the great potential of Central Otago and particularly of Queenstown in mind, he formed a company with two other enthusiasts. Together they built a hangar and office on the Frankton aerodrome, doing the work themselves. From that base, whilst constantly bombarding officialdom with arguments in favour of the establishment of feeder services from the outlying districts to the National Airways Corporation centres, Popeye and his colleagues filled the interim with a variety of services of borderline legitimacy.

Among the most important and novel of these were airlifts of fish and whitebait from the isolated West Coast, supply dropping for trampers, voluntary rescue work, scenic and charter flights, aerial topdressing and seed sowing for farmers; and they were later able to persuade the Wildlife Department that it would pay to drop deercullers, hut materials, and poisoned bait for rabbit extermination in the more inaccessible regions of the back country.

Air Department proved a more stubborn nut to crack, but the time came when Southern Scenic Airways had half a dozen planes working feeder lines to various NAC centres, and were operating a full Queenstown-Dunedin-Queenstown service.

But that was after they had overcome all the difficulties and frustrations of pioneering. Owing to the company's inability to squeeze from the Post Office Department a licence to install a radio telephone network, that would in particular provide on-the-spot weather reports on what were so often widely-differing conditions on either side of the Alps, three of their aeroplanes came to grief in the very first year. Fortunately no lives were lost, but financially it was a drastic setback.

And this is where Popeye's wife Lorie comes into the picture. Of course she was in *his* picture long before that; their eldest son David was born soon after they came to live in Queenstown. But you will be meeting this wonderful person, Lorie, shortly and you will see for yourself that, as well as supporting her husband in all his undertakings, eking out the budget in thin times with various enterprises of her own, helping the children with correspondence-school lessons when later the Lucases took over Cecil Peak station, and so on and on to this final venture, she is also a most charming woman.

If you want the fuller story behind this very brief sketch of two colourful personalities, then read *Popeye Lucas, Queenstown*. The chapter about some of his scenic and chartered flights over the High Alps makes particularly absorbing reading.

The epic story of the vintage buses that take us now 2.4 kilometres from wharf to homestead however, demands a word here. Until a very few years ago all the stations around the lakes were completely dependent upon the *Earnslaw*, not only for farm and domestic supplies, but also for the outgoing delivery of their store sheep and cattle and the annual woolclip. I remember on more than one occasion being on the steamer with livestock as travelling companions. They were penned on the top deck, though in the case of a sizable herd or flock, a special freight trip would be made and most of the ship given over to their accommodation.

When it came to shipping a bus over to Cecil Peak however, the Railways Department—to whom the *Earnslaw* then belonged—refused permission on the ground that the wharf was not sufficiently strong to land it on. Of the delays and obstructions that followed you may read in Popeye's autobiography; sufficient here to say that with his usual unconquerability he determined by some means or other to bring this bus on to the property—and also the equally-full bus

One of the Lucas sons demonstrates sheep-handling with dogs. *National Publicity Studios*

there in front of us. By pick and shovel—after the tractor had gone over a bluff—and a concerted family effort in which Lorie, as usual, took part, he cut a track of sorts around those seemingly-impassable Bayonet Peaks. Over this he finally drove the bus from the neighbouring wharf at Halfway Bay, where the Department had consented to land it. Two days were spent in getting it over the Lochy River, six more in ·driving it over the worst mile, and ten for the entire operation. With characteristic understatement Popeye describes the vehicle upon arrival at the station as being "rather scratched and dented in places, with one or two indicators smashed or buckled, a few broken windows, and minus both rearguards, but otherwise beautifully roadworthy".

When the first bus proved inadequate for the ever-increasing volume of tourists, they brought in the second bus the same way.

Though on the western side a riding track joins each of the lake homesteads to its neighbours, there is still no road access to either the head or the foot of the lake. The situation must therefore have seemed desperate when a few years ago the Railways Department decided to sell the *Earnslaw* because it wasn't paying its way after the opening of the Glenorchy road on the eastern side. But as usual Mr Lucas came up with the right solution, and the station now runs its own barge. Another recent purchase, making the enterprise now entirely selfcontained, was that of their own launch *Viking* for the tourist service.

Since it had already gone to press before the steamer ceased serving the stations, these last developments do not appear in the autobiography.

Perhaps we can hope for a sequel?

What the author is too modest to mention in his book either, is the warmth and friendliness that greet the visitor on arrival at the homestead. There is the hostess, calm and competent, pouring tea from a beautiful old silver service for those who have already alighted. Daughter or daughter-in-law will be handing round fresh buttered scones and homemade jam, and perhaps one of the sons will lend a hand. The others will be occupied with any of the hundred-and-one jobs to be done on a high-country run.

For this is a family concern, and it speaks volumes for the parents that all four boys, grown up now, have decided to remain on the farm. "It's in the blood," says Popeye, who was him-self a farmer's son, and who perhaps has had

difficulty in deciding which was his first love, the air or the land.

You take your tea—well, just anywhere you like: to one of the garden tables shaded by sun umbrellas, to the lawn under one of the lovely old English trees, or you perhaps wander off, cup in hand, to enjoy the glorious outlook from the open side of the secluded valley where the old stone homestead has stood the rigorous winters and sometimes blistering summers of more than a hundred years.

The homestead itself is not particularly large, but when you go indoors, as Mrs Lucas will presently invite you to do, you'll sense the indefinable charm of a place that has been furnished to express its owners' own personality, and is loved and tended with care.

Morning tea on the terrace at Cecil Peak includes scones made by Lorie or Popeye.
National Publicity Studios

You sit in the attractive family livingroom, chatting with your hostess or with one and another of the many visitors, whom it is fun to "spot"—mostly by their voices. They are largely Australians and Americans, some New Zealanders, a few Japanese; and, the last time I went, an intriguing family of Indians sat beside me in the launch.

Mr Lucas himself will presently reappear to tell you, with the aid of panoramic and aerial maps of the whole vast acreage, something of the way in which a high-country station is worked, and to delight his audience with the dry wit he brings to the task.

As a final touch, while you trundle down the road through the hay paddocks on the return trip to the wharf, either he or one of the sons will send the dogs out after a small flock of sheep kept near the homestead—the main flock will be scattered miles away on summer country— to demonstrate the fascinating work these collies do, and the wonderful *rapport* between such dogs and their masters.

If you have enjoyed your brief visit and feel it would be pleasant to stay for a time in so peaceful a spot, Mr and Mrs Lucas have anticipated your wish by renovating the interiors of some old shepherds' cottages for rental. Or if you prefer it, you might stay in the house in rooms set aside for the purpose, and for a few days be one of this unusually happy family, reading or talking, riding or walking, hunting or fishing, or just pottering about in the mountain air.

Those who stay at Cecil Peak as house-guests speak in glowing terms of the Lucas *cuisine*. Without being pretentious or elaborate it is really excellent—and no wonder, for both Lorie and Popeye have a sturdy belief in the virtues of good New Zealand fare cooked with traditional country skills. (At the time of writing this, they are collaborating on a book of New Zealand country cookery.)

"Come again, won't you?" Farewell to Cecil Peak.
A.H. & A.W. Reed Collection

Shortly before publication of this book it was learnt that the Lucases intended to dispose of Cecil Peak by public auction. Whether or not this has indeed happened the story of Popeye Lucas and Cecil Peak is sure to remain relevant reading for any visitor to Queenstown.

6

MORE LAKE EXCURSIONS

THE STORY of shipping on the lake is a long one. Exclusive of the numerous odd craft hastily improvised by the miners themselves, there were in the roaring sixties as many as thirty steamers and sailing vessels—eight of which belonged to the the police.

Among the schooners and ketches, the more interesting names that have been preserved are *Lady of the Lake*, *Morning Star*, *May Queen*, *Moa*, *Mystery*. . . . The first small woodburning steamers were the *Nugget* and the *Expert*. The *Venus* was a steam launch larger than any motor vessel now on the lake.

Some of these craft were imported from overseas, but it was not long before vessels were being built on Wakatipu itself, at the mouth of the Greenstone, with beech milled at Kinloch. Two of these, the paddle-steamers *Wakatipu* and *Antrim*, were launched as early as 1863 and 1866 respectively.

The screw-steamer *Jane Williams*, built on the foreshore of Queenstown Bay in 1874, has a special appeal because of the origin of her name. The story was told me by Miss Mulholland, grand-niece of the owner and daughter of the skipper. As an orphaned boy of eight living with his Aunt Jane in Cornwall, young Williams had apparently already decided on his future career; when his stern aunt was about to chastise him for some misdemeanour, he vanquished her with the remark, "If you don't whip me I'll call my first ship after you." And he kept his word—in faraway New Zealand in 1874.

This ship was later bought by the Wakatipu Steamship Company, who changed her name to *Ben Lomond*, and as such she is remembered by many people still living in Queenstown. By the turn of the century the ranks were thinning, but

Mystery, one of the ketches that plied the lake before the steamboats came in. *Lakes District Museum*

By 1880 *Venus*, "a steam-launch larger than any motor vessel now on the lake", was the pride of the Queenstown fleet. *Lakes District Museum*

Above: *Mountaineer,* built in 1874, ended her days as a
houseboat at Walter Peak station in 1933.
Alexander Turnbull Library

Below: Grand old Lady of the Lake, *Earnslaw.* After 50 years
of sterling service for New Zealand Railways, in 1968 she
seemed doomed by road transport competition – but the
tourist demand earned her a reprieve. *Preston Collection*

both *Ben Lomond* and the paddle-steamer *Mountaineer*—also built in 1874—were still on the lake when in 1911 the Railways Department purchased all privately-owned service shipping. Shortly afterwards *Earnslaw* made her debut, taking over entirely the freight, passenger and also the runholder and tourist mail services to and from the railhead at Kingston. The others mainly plied between Queenstown and the Frankton wharf.

In spite of increasing competition from road services, it was some years before the smaller steamers went out of action. The last of them, the *Mountaineer*, was sold in 1933 to Colonel McKenzie of Walter Peak station. There, moored in the bay, she was used as a houseboat.

Earnslaw alone remained, but intimations of her fate were spelled out when first the south road was opened and, later, the road to Glenorchy.

It is only ten years since the difficult task of linking Glenorchy with Queenstown was finally accomplished. But what was undoubtedly a boon to the township and the farming district at the head proved a last blow to *Earnslaw*. She was now in competition with road services both north and south, and there was little doubt which would win. In 1968 the Railways Department decided to cut their losses and scrap her. Fortunately a small private company, encouraged by a prolonged public outcry by no means locally confined, decided to take over and risk a continuing service, though on much more limited lines. Understandably, the new programme included neither the Kingston run, nor that daylong trip to the head of the lake and back that had given so much joy to so many for so long.

There was something very special about that voyage. The excitement and bustle as the passengers boarded and settled themselves on decks and below, the gay goodbyes from the wharf, were a little like the last minutes before an ocean liner takes to sea. Except for the inevitable groups of trampers bound for regions far beyond the head, perhaps a gang of shearers or a load of stores to be disembarked at one of the homesteads en route, most of the voyagers would be going either to the Routeburn via Kinloch, or to Paradise via Glenorchy. They would be away no more than twelve hours, but it was an adventure, just the same.

Although she no longer travels so far afield,

there's plenty of life left in *Earnslaw*. Boasting two sets of triple-expansion steam engines, she was built for the Railways Department in Dunedin, brought in parts by waggon to the foot of the lake, and there reassembled for launching in 1912. She is said to be the only lake steamer operating in the southern hemisphere, her passenger capacity is something over 1700—soon to be increased—and her speed 22.5 kilometres per hour. At sixty years old she is still spry and hasn't "let herself go" but retires to the slips every winter for a facelift. Last season (1973-74) she reappeared with increased passenger capacity, plus bar facilities for the thirsty.

Earnslaw has recently changed hands again; she now belongs to Fiordland Travel Limited, a company with wide interests in southern scenic resorts. During the winter and spring seasons their large launch *Fiordlander* takes over from the steamer the comparatively short runs they find it economical to run on Wakatipu.

The longest of these takes you to White Point, a spur at the elbow between the middle and north reaches of the lake, from which opens up an incomparable panorama of snowy peaks beyond the head. The route is by Walter Peak and Mount Nicholas stations, the latter the largest of all the Wakatipu runs, all of which however, are between 24 000 and 40 000 hectares.

This is an afternoon cruise, but the brief stop you've made at Walter Peak station on Beach Bay may move you to return to this lovely spot with leisure to see all that it has to offer, for the steamer also runs a morning trip to Walter Peak only.

This was the home of several generations of the McKenzie family, beginning with the first Hugh who came to New Zealand in 1878, and ending with Hugh McKenzie & Sons, who sold the run, as I remember, a few years after the end of the Second World War. The land is still used for its original farming purposes, but the present owner and his predecessor have also developed at the homestead an attractive tourist enterprise. A number of the McKenzie houses, set against the high crags of Walter Peak amongst immense old trees in well-kept grounds, are still standing. You will have tea in one of those nearest the lake, and the one formerly occupied by Colonel Hugh is now a many-roomed museum of furnishings and fashions of the pioneer period,

Earnslaw noses her way in to Walter Peak station, where visitors are welcomed to the old McKenzie estate. *National Publicity Studios*

attractively arranged by Wendy Minshull, one of our local artists. Outdoors there are various farming displays, and a sheep-shearing demonstration. Here under the willows weeping into the bay is the spot where the houseboat *Mountaineer* lay moored for many years. And there at the wharf is *Earnslaw*, white paint and red funnel gleaming in the sun, waiting to take you back to the town you can plainly see across 13 kilometres of dancing water.

A third item on *Earnslaw*'s daily summer programme is a short cruise to the outlet of the lake at the Kawarau bridge in the Frankton Arm. A smorgasbord luncheon is served on board.

The launches *Moana* and *Muratai*, both of which have been on the lake for as long as I can remember, also run trips to Walter Peak twice daily.

In a less sophisticated age these two launches used to take passengers picnicking to Bob's Cove, a bushclad retreat close to White's Point. On the Queenstown side you'll notice in passing a shallow stream, the Twelve-Mile, emerging from a gorge out of all proportion to its size. Son One and I once boarded *Muratai* at this spot in quite

an unorthodox manner. We had planned to walk to Bob's Cove, taking in on the way a small lake we'd not so far seen, and to return on the picnic launch. Lake Dispute—a good spot for rainbow trout—is about 3 kilometres in from the road, but after seeing it, instead of returning by the track, we thought to take a short cut to the cove. We soon became bushed in brow-high bracken and manuka, and by the time we'd fought a way down to the deep bed of the Twelve-Mile our watches warned us that the launch would now be leaving. So we hurried down to the rivermouth, lit a smoky bracken fire and did a kind of dervish dance on the beach—which together succeeded in attracting the attention of the passing *Muratai*.

But then came the real punishment for the tramper's sin of leaving the track: the launch-master doubtless came as far inshore as he dared, but even so we had to wade out waist-deep and suffer the indignity of climbing a rope ladder and being hauled over the gunwales, torn and dripping, in front of all those curious eyes.

There are several other tourist boats on the lake, catering for a variety of interests. For the speed fan there's the hydrofoil *Meteor*, a large covered speedboat on winglike foils, which runs short twenty-minute trips or, alternatively, what is known as the Snowline cruise, which during a run of one and a half hours reveals most of the main features of the middle and north reaches.

The bright red launch *Viking* conducts the twice-daily excursion to Cecil Peak station, of which I've already written. And a much-felt need for a service to the stations not connected with Queenstown by road has recently been filled by the tug *MV Waiomana*; it leaves at 9 am on Wednesdays and Fridays. In a humbler way this takes the place of the former *Earnslaw* trip, and on request the master will take trampers to such starting points as Elfin Bay, Greenstone, and Kinloch, for those wonderful walks in the wilds which I only wish I had space to include in this short book.

Another launch to appear on the lake recently is the fifty-passenger *Kingston Cruiser* which, as its name implies, concentrates on the south end of the lake and works in conjunction with the *Kingston Flyer* rail service—to which I shall introduce you in a later section.

While there's reasonably good fishing round the shores—those monster trout at the pier are sacrosanct, by the way—best results are to be had by trolling at the mouths of the incoming rivers. For those without their own transport the small cabin cruiser *Bellbird* will provide it— fishing gear as well if desired. She's available for charter all day, though early morning and evening are of course the favoured fishing times.

For the plutocratic, both fishing and hunting safaris are run from Mount Creighton station, lasting one or more days as arranged.

It would be pleasant if I could end by recommending, as a contrast to all this communal activity, a quiet drift on the harbour in a dinghy, alternating with a little vigorous exercise on the oars. Alas, the fleet of small open boats that when idle were formerly to be found lying here on the shingle, have been put out of action by those little U-drive speedsters. There's the depot, just beside the jetty where the private speedboats are launched. Would you care to have a go?

Visitors disembarking at Walter Peak. Among the many attractions here are a pioneer museum and displays of farming techniques, including sheep-shearing. *National Publicity Studios*

Angling in tranquil waters, from a beach at Walter Peak. *National Publicity Studios*

7

ON THE RIVERS

FOR THRILLS WITHOUT SPILLS let me recommend a short trip down the Shotover in Trevor and Heather Gamble's Hamilton jet. Though perfectly safe, the experience will make you think lightly of being shot into space from a rocket.

The takeoff place is at Arthurs Point. Almost any hour of the day you may catch the Shotover Jet bus beside the Mount Cook office, or you may drive your own car the same 6.4 kilometres through the Queenstown gorge—here known simply as "the gorge".

This is the route that Thomas Arthur made famous when he and his mate went prospecting to the Shotover that Sunday afternoon in 1862, and the road still necessarily winds over the original trail of the diggers who promptly followed them. Soon there were hundreds of their horses grazing the gorge, and it was declared a commonage for the purpose.

This flatter part near the Queenstown end, into which several streams run off the steeps on either side, was not always given over to bog-rush and buttercup; it began to silt up as a result of all the sluicing and blasting that later took place on the eastern cliffs. In a corner of our garden in the gorge we have a shed known as the magazine, where materials were stored for the purpose. Its concrete-lined walls are inches thick, and the white-pine interior is scribbled over with warnings relating to the safe storage of gelignite and detonators. They are variously dated in the first decade of this century, when new methods of mining rejuvenated the waning industry for a further few years.

Beyond this point where the swamp ends and the cliffs slope down into milder but always rising country, the gorge narrows a little before meeting the Shotover. A side track beyond that gate on the right leads round the river bluffs to an abandoned sluicing claim at the back of Queenstown Hill, which fills all the space between the two gorges. . . . No, you'd have to go on foot; it's little more than a bridle track.

About five minutes' drive past the gate the road dips sharply to the Arthurs Point hotel. If you look over the bank before going down you'll see, far below, the Shotover whirling between rocky walls. In just a few minutes you'll be whirling there too.

Behind its effective modern facade the old stone inn at the foot of the hill still stands, the last of many. One wonders how this narrow shelf could have accommodated also the Gold Receiver's office, the livery-and-bait stables, and several more pubs. Many of these last however, were stationed over the bridge a few chains further on.

The precise spot at which Arthur pegged out the claim from which he later took a fortune is not known, but just over the bridge spanning the river at its narrowest, a cairn built of local stone commemorates his initial find "at a place near here". This was almost certainly on the opposite side of the road, where for a short distance the oft-confined river has found room to wander, and the comparatively low banks are thick with blackberry-covered tailings.

It was on these banks and beaches that all signs of the first diggings were swept away in 1863 together with many of the diggers themselves, in a flood whose magnitude has not since been equalled. Strange that it should have occurred in the very first year. It would almost seem that the gods resented this sudden invasion of their fastnesses, but once having seen that it would take more than disaster to discourage the gold lust, they apparently gave up.

There's a depot down there among the blackberries, and below it the jetboat—if you've timed your arrival well—is emptying its previous load of passengers. When you arrive on the beach, pause to look not only downstream where the beautiful bridge spanning the gorge invites the eye to rest for long moments, but also upstream where from another of its gorges the river emerges at speed to continue in more leisurely and meandering fashion through a wide sandy basin. It was from the mouth of this upper gorge, temporarily blocked with debris brought down by the flood, that the pent-up waters burst suddenly upon the

Junction Hotel, Arthurs Point. "Behind its modern facade this old stone inn still stands" — the last of many. *National Publicity Studios*

unsuspecting diggers sleeping beside their claims on these banks and beaches during that fatal night in the spring of 1863.

Though running high today, the milky teal-green river carries no burden of uprooted trees on its swiftly moving current, and as he helps you into the boat Trevor Gamble's cheerful, burring Southland voice is doubly reassuring—until you catch that glint of mischief in his eye. Too late. Almost before the last passenger is seated, the boat has shot under the bridge and is careering in mad fashion down the gorge, rocking, swirling, shooting from side to side, seeming at times to miss the rocky walls by only a hair.

It's mostly contrived, of course, but this audacious, incredibly dexterous handling of the boat to create an illusion of fierce whirlpools and rapids where only mild ones exist, certainly adds to the fun. But don't let the shrieks and laughter put you off observing the gorge itself, these great walls of clean-sliced rock rearing to show little more than a slit of sky between them. And you haven't much time to take in their stark beauty before the jet is out of the gorge

and bouncing along a staider reach of the river known as Big Beach.

If its owner is a little proud of his wonderfully controllable craft, he is prouder still of Bill Hamilton, the New Zealander who developed the first of its kind. He will tell you that although at least two Americans have since patented somewhat similar boats, the only one to have so far negotiated the tricky Colorado River upstream as well as down, is a Hamilton jet.

Mr Gamble's *Shotover* is designed to carry eight passengers, has a draught of only 89 millimetres and can travel at speeds up to 70 kilometres an hour. She's made of an aluminium alloy eight times as strong as fibreglass, so that even if the unlikely happened, she would just bounce off the rock again without any worse consequence than raising the passengers' temperatures a little.

It's a happy accident that the *Shotover* could be so aptly named. The river itself was at first called the Tummel by the Scot who was the first European to discover it, but when Mr Rees took up the run through which it flows he renamed it after his partner's home in England, Shotover Park—rather a sad alteration for those of us who've walked "the road to the Isles".

This Big Beach that you're rapidly passing was the richest piece of ground on what for more than thirty years was accepted as the richest river in the world. Only when gold was discovered on the Alaskan Klondike in 1896 did the Shotover have to step down into second place.

More than a ton of gold was taken from Big Beach, much of it latterly by Sew Hoy, a Chinese who reworked it during the dredging boom shortly before and after the turn of this century. (Mr Sew Hoy continued to live on in Queenstown, and his family dispersed from here only a few years ago.) There on the right just before the jet shoots into a second gorge, you can see the remains of the rusty old dredge,

Below: *Shotover Jet* carries eight at 70 km/h. She is a descendant of the Hamilton jets that made the first upstream ascent of the Colorado River, USA. *National Publicity Studios*

buried up to its arms in sand and gravel.

A dozen or two of the gigantic loose-lying slabs in this gorge would pave the Mall. But on the whole it is less impressive than the first, there's more talk and fewer thrills, and in a few minutes after emerging the point of return is reached at Tucker Beach, nearly 8 kilometres from the bridge.

Why the name? Because here the takings were not so spectacular, and a digger had to work hard for his tucker.

The entire sprint there and back is accomplished in less than half an hour but, before landing, Trevor will probably run you almost to the mouth of that up-river gorge mentioned earlier in connection with the great flood. What you've come to see however is a different type of flood gushing from the mouth of a tunnel on the left.

This 240 metre tunnel was dug through the rock in 1906 to divert the river from its natural bed. Although in early summer when the snows are melting there's water enough to make both river and tunnel appear pretty formidable, in winter—which was when riverbed miners always won their best returns—the tunnel would take most if not all of the volume.

The jet trip is apparently a winning card; already the next group of passengers is waiting on the landing. But there's another, one more worthy to be called a cruise, also on the Shotover, and leaving from the same Tucker Beach that is the jet's terminus.

This *Kon-Tiki* raft trip is also a husband-and-wife enterprise. Mr Tinker is a Kiwi, his wife an American, and it was while they were floating down the Colorado on a rubber raft that they conceived the idea of bringing one of these unusual crafts out to New Zealand. The whole structure is inflatable and looks like a series of huge rubber tyres refashioned into the shape of a boat. It is 4.8 metres long and about half as wide amidships, safely accommodates ten, and resembles a raft in that it simply floats flat on the water and drifts along.

Of course its great virtue, to the oldies in particular, is that it makes no sound as it moves gently with the current; nor does it demand instant observation if one hopes to store in mind anything of the passing scene. To ensure good visibility for all, the *Kon Tiki* travels not

"Fossicking." Young and old alike hire goldpans and try their luck. Some of them do find a little "colour", even now.
Alexander Turnbull Library

busy to take a bow, you'll be enchanted to see not only crowds of black-backed gulls but also small groups or lone specimens of the less gregarious wading birds: dotterels, plovers, and the pied oystercatcher. And just before the raft reaches its destination by the Lower Shotover bridge, a flock of wood-pigeons will almost invariably fly out of the crevices of a certain cliff on the west bank. Since the whitish markings on the almost sheer face can't possibly be droppings, Mr Tinker's theory is that the birds use this unlikeliest of places in which to find the honey-eating pigeons, for filing their beaks—which apparently keep on growing just as our fingernails do. There were only four birds the day James and I saw this remarkable phenomenon, but Mr Tinker says that at times he has seen as many as a hundred or so.

Since the beginning and end of this trip are

bow-first like most self-respecting boats, but sideways like a crab.

Although these lower reaches of the river are comparatively mild—no gorges at all between Tucker Beach and the mouth—the current must still be treated with respect. At 13 kilometres an hour it travels faster than an Olympic walker, and since the soft banks of mica schist in varying states of disintegration constantly invite it to change its course, dislodged debris and new shallows form mild hazards which the skipper controls with a pair of quietly moving oars. The inconstant volume of water and frequent changes of course due to flooding make the Shotover a good bet for the present-day craze known as fossicking. You never know when some secret lucky crevice might at last be exposed, or when gold borne down on a flood from higher country might be deposited in the sands and gravels on the upstream side of a jutting rock. Tucker Beach—always a pleasant picnicking spot—is now one of the more favoured areas for this serious pastime. Daily during the summer holidays young and old are to be seen searching, or with shovel and dish hopefully panning, in these likely places. (You may hire a goldpan from a small shop in Beach Street.)

One of the most interesting features of this hour-long drift downriver is the birdlife on its shorelike islands and banks. Unless engaged in early summer nesting when they're mostly too

Kawarau Gorge. How much gold still lies beneath this old suspension bridge? *National Publicity Studios*

46

Passengers on the *Kon Tiki* inflated raft drift quietly and easily, and have time to observe the plentiful birdlife of the river. At the right season they may see, among many other species, this pied oystercatcher nesting in the shingle. *National Publicity Studios*

necessarily in different places, the raft travels—on a trailer—with the van that takes passengers from and back to Queenstown. While you've been drifting down the river Mrs Tinker has been driving from Tucker Beach to the terminus about a mile from the mouth, has backed the trailer to the water's edge ready to receive the raft, and prepared a cup of tea, which upon arrival you drink at a pleasant spot on the bank.

Then it's all aboard the van you go, skipper and raft inclusive, to be driven back to Queenstown.

A second jet service takes passengers via the Frankton Arm for a short distance down the Kawarau. Whilst very much larger than its Shotover tributary, the Kawarau is a much more tranquil river—at least in its upper reaches. Until a fatal accident occurred in the rapids of its gorge some few years ago, this was a really exciting adventure, covering 40 kilometres in all, of everchanging scene and hazard. Still, for those familiar with neither the arm nor the river, this can still be a rewarding trip. I know of no more beautiful stretch of water in the world than this broad, bottle-green, majestically-moving mile or so before the river turns to flow round the base of the Remarkables; nor can the rich farmlands rolling gently away from its northern bank be outmatched by many.

They did not always appear so prosperous. When Gilbert Rees first came this way the entire valley was covered with matakouri. With his usual penchant for descriptive names the Maori called the river, also the mountains above it,

Kawarau, meaning small shrub. For once, I think, the Pakeha chose in the Remarkable Mountains a better name for this jagged range.

There beyond the first short stretch of the river, is the takeoff spur from which most of our family have at one time and another climbed the Remarkables. Son Two has done so twice, having been beaten at first on the final 90 metres of the highest peak of the triple cone, for lack of an ice-axe. Next time he took care to go in high summer.

Although ignored by those who always speak of "the double cone", the third and southernmost one is actually the highest—2339 metres.

About 5 kilometres down river, the Kawarau is joined by the first of its tributaries, a sadly tamed Shotover wandering aimlessly through sandy flats, unrecognisable as the hearty cataract that swept us through the gorge at Arthurs Point. Let's not linger over the sight of this degeneration. It's time to turn back.

Old homestead, Arthurs Point. Cool in summer's heat, snugly warm in winter, these old stone buildings are a feature of Lake County. *Alexander Turnbull Library*

Right: An early view of the Arthurs Point hotel. On this narrow shelf were perched several taverns, a livery-and-bait stables, a bank and a gold-receiver's office.
Lakes District Museum

Below: On the road to Arrowtown. "There is excellent farmland on these middle downs", in this case those of Thurlby Domain.
Alexander Turnbull Library

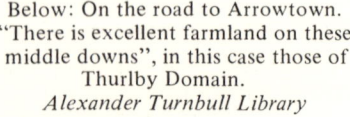

8

ARROWTOWN

THERE ARE two main roads to Arrowtown, with nothing much to choose between them. One is a bare half-mile longer than the other, and both pass through rich farmlands in downlike valleys with a scattered range of hills dividing them. For myself I can never decide which is the more delightful drive, but if your base is in Queenstown the simple solution is to go one way and return the other. For those dependent on public transport, an H & H bus does this very thing, leaving every afternoon at 2 o'clock.

You've already been through the gorge to Arthurs Point and over the bridge. From there you climb to a small plateau, so that now you're riding high above Big Beach where the old dredge lies. On the right of the road you pass a relic of the gold era, a one-time coaching inn which has been restored and is now a restaurant, the Packer's Arms. It was one of twenty-two pubs between Arthurs Point and the Skippers road corner. It's about 8 kilometres from Queenstown, and they dine and wine you well in the very attractive interior. Like its opposite neighbour a little farther on, it is built of stone.

This second stone building is a two-storey house with three window gables across the front. It once raised my temperature to such a pitch that I tried, without success, to buy it.

That was years ago, before we bought the property in the gorge. But the family has not yet allowed me to live down my experiences during that abortive period when I tramped all over the countryside in search of a holiday house. Just *any* kind of house, so long as it was stone. In my then state of crazed enthusiasm, such trifling defects as a tumbled chimney, broken window-panes, even a breach in the walls, had no power to deter me.

Reactions to my persistence were various. Not every farmer figuratively slammed the door in my face, and only one did so literally. The only common factor was the peculiar expression, a kind of shocked caution, registered by all at the sight of a dishevelled woman on their doorsteps hopefully requesting that they sell their stone barns—generally in use—or their old abandoned houses. It dawned upon me only gradually that while listening to my pleas they were mentally reaching for the telephone to warn the police that a madwoman was abroad.

There were two, however, who took me seriously enough to say that yes, I could have the old barn, but on one condition: I must buy the farm along with it!

Well, we couldn't afford a farm, nor did we really want one. So that was that.

The stone house with the gabled windows stands at a junction. The road left runs up to Skippers and the ski fields on Coronet Peak, while that to the right goes dashing down almost to river level, then takes an upward leap before it disappears intriguingly into the hills. It's a temptation to which you could do worse than fall, and it too will eventually lead you by a network of secondary roads to Arrowtown.

There is some excellent farmland on these middle downs, and another notable stone house, also two-storeyed, but in sad disrepair. This is Thurlby Domain. The land was taken up and the house built in the "roaring sixties" by a German who prospered by selling mercery to the miners. Later he established branches of the business in all the main centres, where HB for Hallenstein Bros is still a very familiar trademark. There are now fifty HB branches throughout New Zealand.

Thurlby has for many years belonged to Mr Ron Gordon, and if you ask him politely—at the new house a few hundred yards further on—he will allow you to wander in the one-time garden whose present delight is its ancient trees.

Mr Gordon told me an interesting story about one of these trees. *Cretagus mollis* was a new name to me, and I think the tree is very rare in this country. It is a native of Canada, and it seems that some years ago a certain wheat blight for which the *Cretagus* tree was host, became so uncontrollable that the Canadian government ordered the destruction of all such trees throughout the country. After a lapse of time, when the

Once a gay and gracious home, built by one of the Hallenstein brothers who founded the chain of "HB" stores, Thurlby Domain is now a heartbreaking ruin. *Ron Gordon*

pest had been eradicated, it was decided that the exterminated species must be restored. So a request was sent out via the press throughout the world for seeds of the *Cretagus* tree. And the only reply, plus a quantity of seed, came from Thurlby Domain, Queenstown, New Zealand.

We ourselves have had occasion to be grateful to Mr Gordon. My favourite berberis grew from a Thurlby cutting, and the stone foundations of the house we eventually built in the gorge were originally an outbuilding in the Thurlby orchard that was known as the jam factory. Our benefactor would take no recompense; it cost us nothing more than the labour of dismantling, and a deal of dust in the eyes from the pug with which the slabs were held together. This pug, a sticky kind of local clay, was the only form of cement used in all these old dry-stone walls and buildings in the Wakatipu district. It was usually mixed with salt.

From Thurlby, so long as you continue in a general easterly direction, you'll arrive by one side road or another at Arrowtown.

Among all the small towns of New Zealand, Arrow is almost the only one to have something of the charm of an old English village. And alone among the former mining towns it seems to have retained without too much selfconsciousness something of the aura of its past. You hardly need to go to the Lake County Museum to be aware of this, though if you do, the feeling will be heightened as you examine the extensive collection of miners' gear, domestic appliances and fashions of the period. Don't be put off by the grim faces of the pioneer inhabitants; remember that in those primitive days of the photographic art, the sitter dared not move so much as an eyelash while the operator waited beneath his funereal tent for long seconds between the press and release of the shutter.

The museum is at the end of the main street,

The old Centennial Museum, Arrowtown, now housed in a stone building donated by the Bank of New Zealand.
National Publicity Studios

Interior of the Arrowtown museum, 1951. Kinglsey Butler, aged 90, was the first white child in the little town and is here demonstrating the use of a miner's "cradle".
National Publicity Studios

Left: The Arrowtown jail. "The cells are small and pitchy-dark."
Free Lance Collection, Alexander Turnbull Library

Below: Arrowtown, perhaps the only small New Zealand town that preserves "something of the charm of an old English village". *National Publicity Studios*

together with two or three vintage stores and one of the original hotels. It was formerly the bank, and has retained on its windows the notice Gold Office; on its stone step is a concavity worn by a generation of heavily-booted feet. Beside the door too, is a simple relic that for me more than anything else raises ghosts from the past: an iron scraper, worn thin in the middle, on which the miners cleaned the mud from their boots before hurrying to deposit the day's harvest within.

I'm not sure that I should recommend your going to see the old stone jail, where malefactors were incarcerated in what seems to our generation the most appalling conditions. Since greed knows no laws and too-close propinquity breeds crime, it's perhaps not surprising that the Arrow diggings, tucked into a hidden corner of the hills in a gorge so narrow that the men scarce had room to swing pick or shovel, should have proved the most lawless on the goldfields. Yet even the worst crimes committed over pirating, claim-jumping and outright theft, would hardly seem to warrant such living-quarters for offenders as those in the grim old building that was once the Arrow jail.

The cells are small and some of them pitchy dark, with no window openings. From my one visit there I can't remember noticing any means of ventilation either, but there must have been something—else the cemetery on the hill would be even more extensive than it is!

It's hard to imagine all the turmoil and urgency of this brief period in the history of what is now one of the most peaceful spots on earth—in spite of its popularity with part-time residents. Like its larger neighbour, Queenstown, though fortunately in a less sophisticated way, Arrowtown now prospers mainly by catering for passing tourists, and more especially for the owners of holiday houses who come for intermittent periods to enjoy summer sun or winter skiing. It has also a certain backing from nearby farms, and there's even the odd miner still fossicking in the river. We might just have the luck to meet one if we go far enough up the gorge.

But first, a cup of coffee? There's a very pleasant place called simply the Stone Cottage, at the near end of that much-photographed row of tiny dwellings toeing the street behind the ancient avenue of English beech, ash and lime trees.

Main Street, Macetown, on a winter's heyday.
Lakes District Museum

Although great quantities of gold were taken out of the Arrow it is quite a small river. The wandering reach below the township terrace is a disappointing sea of gravel, beneath which is said to lie the first small village, inundated by the flood of 1863. But in the gorge a little farther upstream, all is perfection. Here you may find a dozen picnicking spots, little oases of green on the milder left bank, with deep translucent pools beneath the rocky bluffs across the way, ideal for for bathing.

If you were to wander far enough up the gorge you would eventually come to Macetown. A weird tractor-trailer vehicle manages to negotiate a way to this former mining village, but "in our day" we walked: 19 kilometres, twenty-three river crossings and mighty bluffs frowning upon our intrusion all the way. A miner working at the mouth of a tributary called the Billy showed us how to cradle. He was making a living at it, he confided—but obviously not enough to replace his tumbledown hut with a castle.

Macetown itself, under the white caps of the Advance Peaks, has nothing but a stone wall, green turf, some fine English trees and odd bits of garden paving to tell the usual tale. We know well the son of a schoolteacher who taught there when it was a quartz-mining township of more than a thousand inhabitants.

Macetown did not expire so rapidly as did many of the other gold towns of Otago. I like

Main Street, Macetown, where once over 1000 residents promenaded.
Now summer visitors have only the trees to admire and enjoy.
National Publicity Studios

Arrowtown visitors may go on to see ghostly Macetown, travelling in this ingenious tractor-trailer
vehicle, here seen crossing the Arrow River. *National Publicity Studios*

the story of the last twelve men, known locally as the Twelve Apostles, who continued scratching a living from the soil and the river until one by one they were laid away in the cemetery at Arrow. Were they carried out? There was certainly no other way—unless by packhorse, which was the way that all the supplies and all the machinery for mining had over the years been carried in.

But that forgotten little backwater is not for today. To continue on the second lap of the round trip you drive back up the Arrow hill to the junction of the two main roads, now taking that on the left. It leads past Lake Hayes, minute in comparison with Wakatipu, but lovely as a dream—when the weather is right. Cupped in emerald hills planted here and there with grouped trees, the whole encircled again by mountains, it mirrors all on its surface in unbelievable beauty. The Maori called it Waiwhakaata, Water of Reflections.

The buses include in this round trip a visit to the privately-owned Waterfall Park at the east end of the lake. The park is well laid out, and the attractions include pools of trout and a natural waterfall.

It is surely an affront to the memory of a brave man and an undue honour to a bad one, that the name of this lake is wrongly spelled, even on survey maps. It was discovered by Donald Hay, travelling from the south, the year before Rees and von Tunzelmann made their fruitful journey into the interior. At the foot of Lake Wakatipu he found an abandoned Maori raft on which he spent an adventurous fortnight complete with storms, frosts and spills, paddling round its shores.

Finishing his perilous journey at the outlet, Hay climbed the Peninsula hill and from there saw the enticing country away to the east. In spite of dwindling resources—by this time he had only his gun and his wits to provide sustenance in a land whose only edible creatures were at that time birds and eels—he left the *mokihi* (raft) and hastened down the valley as far as this dimple in the downs, which should therefore bear his name rather than that of the notorious Bully Hayes who spent a turbulent year or two at the Arrow settlement and whose name would better have graced its jail.

Not until he reached the lake he'd seen from the hill did hunger drive Donald Hay back to the homestead of the runholder in the south from which he'd set out on his epic journey.

The sequel to the tale is a sad anticlimax. When he returned to Dunedin to take out a depasturing licence to the splendid valley of his choice he found that someone in the Lands and Survey office, who'd never so much as stirred from his chair, had already claimed it.

The brief relation of Donald Hay's story has brought us almost unaware to the Lower Shotover bridge, whose basement you saw from the *Kon-Tiki* raft. From there you're on familiar ground: the green Frankton flats, Frankton itself, the road round the Arm, the last long hill and—home.

Lake Hayes, called by the Maoris Waiwakaata, the Water of Reflections. It was named after the pioneer Donald Hay, not the notorious Bully Hayes.
National Publicity Studios

"For Experienced Drivers Only." The Skippers Road in horse-and-buggy days, but it is no wider now.
Alexander Turnbull Library

"The scant remains... sometimes nothing more than a chimney, a broken wall, or a grove of exotic trees." Hereford cattle graze by what was once a miner's home. *Alexander Turnbull Library*

9

SKIPPERS CANYON

I FIRST HEARD of Skippers when I was quite a small child. My parents had returned from a holiday in a little village called Queenstown, and the they had a hair-raising story to tell of a certain drive they'd taken while there, in a coach-and-six. At one stage of the journey a wheel had gone over what appeared to be the misty depths of a bottomless ravine. My admiration of the driver who crept to the head of the inside leader was intense, but my sympathies were with the passengers, whom he cautioned not to panic but to alight one by one on the near side and to slip to the rear through the narrow corridor between coach and bluff.

By what miracle the driver managed to keep the horses under control and get that dangling wheel back on the road I know not, but all survived to tell the tale.

That there have not been any fatal accidents on the Skippers road is probably due to the impossibility of speeding upon it. Even those who disregard the sign at the turnoff "For Experienced Drivers Only", soon discover its wisdom. But as the driver, however experienced, is unlikely to take his eyes off the road to enjoy something of the wonders around him, most people prefer to trust themselves to the bus drivers, who have been over the road—not its edge!—twice a day for years. Occasionally vehicles have gone over, but never with fatal results. During the severe winters experienced in this high alpine country the road is often closed to wheeled traffic.

I always feel that the brochures advertising Skippers should quote Robert Louis Stevenson's line about travelling hopefully being better than to arrive. It can't be too much stressed that the drive itself is the attraction. Although Skippers Point—named after a Captain Duncan, always known as the Skipper—is a pleasant enough place, it must disappoint those who imagine the goal must always be the climax of any journey. In this case, the journey itself is the thing.

It was not until 1923 that motor traffic was allowed to use this road at all, and then only after much local dispute and a final decision by the court. Since it serves only four homesteads and because of the engineering difficulties involved in making a new one, the road remains much the same as when it was built by the gold-seekers over a century ago.

Not that it was a poor effort. The wonder is that with nothing but handtools and human determination they conquered that series of stubborn bluffs and cross-gullies that would surely have daunted lesser men. Their beautifully canted bastion walls of local rock are especially admirable.

But it is still a one-way road built originally for horse traffic, in particular for the strings of packhorses on whose backs all the machinery required for sluicing and quartzmining were laboriously carried. Like nearly all roads in the Lake County it requires constant servicing after bad weather but, perhaps not surprisingly, receives it less promptly than most.

The full 32 kilometres from Queenstown through and beyond the gorge is sometimes called the Skippers Road, but its unique character is not evident until you turn left about 4.8 kilometres from Arthurs Point on the road to Arrowtown. It climbs steeply to the saddle, where a branch leads off to the Coronet ski-fields. Looking back from this point you have a splendid view that includes both the Queenstown and Shotover Gorges, Lake Wakatipu, the Speargrass Flats, the Wharehuanui Downs and, everywhere, the ubiquitous mountains.

Thereafter the way becomes increasingly spectacular, always winding, whether up or down, and hemmed in on either side by ranges lifting in numerous peaks from 1500-2130 metres. From Skippers Saddle you run down the 8 kilometres or so of Long Gully, through the kind of virgin tussock country that strikes a chord in most New Zealand hearts. And strangely enough it is in this comparatively milder country that there are to be seen the striking rocky outcrops bearing for obvious reasons such names as The Lighthouse, Castle Rock, The Hedgehog, Heaven's Gates. The last

Skippers township a few years ago. "Now there is no one
except the runholder and his family."
Alexander Turnbull Library

seems so ready to catch a wheel on either side
that nervous passengers might think it would be
more aptly named the Gates of Hell.

From Pinchers Bluff onwards, following now
the Shotover all the way, the terraces that were
ruthlessly scoured for gold are less attractive,
though the river itself, blue-green and writhing
far below, has beauty enough. At various points
you pass the scant remains of one-time townships
or wayside hotels, sometimes nothing more than
a chimney, a broken wall, or a group of exotic
trees to remind one that these lonely wastes have
a human past.

One of these abandoned settlements however,
has recently had a comeback, if only in a comparatively small way. Just this side of Maori Point
the bus makes a fairly prolonged stop so that you
may watch Mr E.D. Scheib working by hydraulic
elevator the alluvial claim he took up about three
years ago. Mrs Scheib has opened a small shop

containing souvenirs made in part from gold
taken out of the claim. A complimentary cup of
tea provided by the bus service is also taken at
the Scheibs' new home on Sainsbury Terrace.

A little further on is Maori Point Saddle, overlooking the Shotover, the claims of the Skippers
Mining Co., and the old township of Skippers
itself. Here the bus now stops, as the Skippers
bridge is unsuitable for public vehicles, but if you
are on foot or have your own transport, carry on.

About 15 kilometres short of Skippers you
pass—if you're lucky—the Blue Slip, the most
notoriously temperamental of all the trouble-
spots on the road. Hardly a year goes by that a
washout doesn't occur here, sometimes severe
enough to warrant its closing, sometimes
demanding only a little added care in driving. On
one occasion of our taking the family to Skippers
we almost came to grief at this spot. James
calculated that we could get across and so we
did—but with the rear outside wheel jumping a
gap of several inches, as was sickeningly felt, and
after the event plainly seen by the lack of a
wheelmark at that spot on the oozing surface.

For quite a long time mining was carried on
spasmodically at Skippers, and there were also
two or three who stayed on to the end of their
course. The first time we went there Mr

Skippers Hotel and post office during the mining era.
Lakes District Museum

This Maori Point dredge was still working in the 1930s. Sluicing and quartz-crushing were other gold-recovery techniques used in this area. *Alexander Turnbull Library*

Sainsbury was still making a living on Stony Creek; John Aspinall worked a claim on the terrace for fifty-six years; and a Mr Lipton was well over eighty, and comfortably off before he gave in.

But now there is no one at Skippers except the runholder and his family. The homestead comes plainly into view shortly after you cross the suspension bridge, the sturdy structure that looks as though it will remain cabled to the rocks that hold it 100 metres above the river, for at least another century.

Those who have read Terri Macnicol's absorbing book, *Beyond the Skippers Road*, about her experiences as the wife of a high-country runholder will always look upon the Mount Aurum homestead with affection. Her courage and cheerfulness in face of what most of us would consider fearful odds—of which the hazards of the road were not the least—come strongly

through the narration of events that are believable only because told with such obvious sincerity. There is nothing especially grand about the house itself, but its setting of a veritable forest of larch trees backed by white mountains peaks most decidedly is.

I ought not perhaps to have said at the beginning that there's nothing especially attractive about Skippers; this larch forest itself is a delight. One wonders from what land the seed came and who planted the first little group whose progeny have now so generously covered the hills. Some young Scottish miner perhaps, recalling his father's advice to "Aye be stickin' in a tree, lad; it grows while ye're sleepin'." And we ourselves always remember with gratitude that our own small larch grove, already grown to full stature, was planted with tiny seedlings gathered at Mount Aurum.

Near the homestead the buses finally halt, and

Chinese miners entertaining a visitor. Note the skilful loose-stone construction of the outhouse and the chimney made from old tins. *Alexander Turnbull Library*

time is allowed for passengers to see the little that remains of the former settlement: a tumbled hotel, and the small lonely cemetery whose humble stones yet speak so eloquently. There is a custom among the Chinese of leaving money on the grave for the use of their dead in the spirit world, and upon our first visit to Skippers, many years ago, we were astonished to see that several coins on the gravestone of one Hoy Yow had remained untouched by pilfering hands.

On that same occasion we found the Miners' Library was still extant. To encourage this amenity that appeared in almost all the early settlements, the custom was for the Government to provide a subsidy equal to whatever sums the miners themselves could collect. The Skippers folk must have been keen readers, for the iron building housing an extensive collection was as large as most small-town libraries of today. But

by this time the roof had caved in, with the inevitable result that many of the strewn books were at the mercy of the elements. They comprised a wide range of subjects and were mostly bound in half-calf.

James and I and the two friends with whom we'd driven to Skippers spent a long time in that shed, and when eventually we returned to Queenstown and emptied our pockets we found that each of us had been moved—let us hope by compassion for the abandoned—to purloin a book. Perhaps because it is still on our shelves I can remember only the name of James's: *The Works of Josephus*, the Jewish historian.

I hope that when you go to Skippers you'll return with another kind of treasure. During last summer's drought, when the rivers fell to exceptionally low levels, two nuggets were found there weighing 56 and 112 grammes respectively. Ask Mr Scheib to show you how it's done!

60

10

CORONET PEAK

THE NAME WIGLEY is well known throughout New Zealand, but in Queenstown it is a household word. Members of this Canterbury family have contributed very substantially over the last century to its development as a top tourist centre. And the most telling of these contributions has perhaps been the gradual establishment of Coronet Peak as a leading international ski field.

It all began when shortly after the 1914-18 war Rodolph Wigley expanded his already established Mount Cook Transport Company into the Mount Cook—Queenstown Motor Company. Into this business his two sons, Harry and Sandy, came when they left school in the late 1920s. The times were hardly favourable, but although tourism usually falls an early victim to economic recession, the company managed to ride out the worldwide depression of the early 1930s.

Meantime all three Wigley men had learned to fly—father at the age of sixty—and all held commercial licences. In 1935 they bought a small

biplane, on the precarious strength of which they formed an associate company, Queenstown-Mount Cook Airways Ltd. The plane was used mainly for scenic trips based on the then very new aerodrome at Queenstown.

It was while engaged in this service that they "discovered" the splendid ski slopes on Coronet Peak, which only a few local enthusiasts were then using. Born to the outdoor life their father loved, the boys had learned to climb and ski at the Mount Cook Hermitage, where the Transport Company had introduced skiing from Europe as early as 1921. So now a further plan began to take shape, whose implementation would eventually transform Queenstown from a summer-only to an all-seasons holiday resort.

Both it and the longterm plan to run scheduled air services in the area were stalled, however, by the Second World War. In 1946 Rodolph Wigley died, and after their war services in the RNZAF the younger son took up land in Canterbury while Harry Wigley returned to the task of re-

A Rodolph Wigley Darracq service-car of the Mount Cook Transport Company, at Fairlie. He extended his service to Queenstown shortly after the first world war. *Wigley Collection*

Ski-slopes unlimited at Coronet Peak. Road access and lifts enable the skiers to spend most of their day on the snow. *National Publicity Studio*

Coronet chairlift terminal. Queenstown's winter season rivals that of her summer. Here is skiing *de luxe*.
National Publicity Studios

invigorating the understandably neglected road transport business.

Before the end of the decade it had not only recovered but also, under the new name of the Mount Cook & Southern Lakes Company, had extended its lines to link Queenstown, Wanaka, Mount Cook, Timaru and Christchurch; a road had been cut to the Coronet ski field and two rope tows installed, the first in New Zealand. More spectacular development was soon to follow.

Those first tows have since been superseded by more modern means of lifting skiers to take-off heights on the mountain, but it was on one of these that our youngest son spent all his spare cash once he'd graduated from the learners' school on the lower slopes. He alone of the family, having the advantage of beginning at an early age, became sufficiently proficient to race several times in the New Zealand championships—with creditable though not conspicuous success.

The first time James and I went up the mountain we decided cravenly that this was a sport for the young, wonderful to watch but dangerous—and we had so much further to fall than the children! We found it more comfortable to watch through the fieldglasses from our windows in the gorge, the tiny black figures moving in a straight line up the mountain like well-trained ants, then down again in a scatter like rudely disturbed ones.

When we returned after several years, we were astonished to see the changes that had occurred in the interim. Where formerly there had been simply two or three club huts and a service building for the hiring of boots and skis, there was now a veritable village, and the site had been moved to a more commodious shelf a little higher up the mountain.

Since it was midwinter, when it's sometimes necessary to use wheel chains, we'd decided to go in one of the several Mount Cook & Southern Lakes tourist buses which run several times every day to and from the mountain. (This service continues throughout the year, so you needn't wait for winter snows to see at close quarters something of Coronet's attractions. But of course there's much more colour and activity during the ski season, so if at all possible try to go then.)

From the foot of the Skippers road branching off the Arrow highway you travel in low gear all the way, climbing without let-up. At the saddle the Company's well-paved road branches off right, to a height of about 610 metres, where on a long cul-de-sac that was formerly the site of the first ski buildings, many hundreds of cars are parked nose to tail. A last long hairpin bend reveals the new ski village.

It is a village without a street but with a variety of attractive clubhouses, commonrooms, a miscellaneous-goods shop, ski and repair shops, an administrative building, a doctor's surgery, and a handsome restaurant on two levels, the upper one a large open-air room provided with seats, tables and chairs. Three-course meals, grills, salads, morning and afternoon teas are served throughout the day, also takeaway

At Coronet Peak, Rodolph and his sons were pioneers of skiing, as well as of motor and air transport. *Wigley Collection*

lunches to be eaten in the commonroom or on the balcony.

Hundreds of people will be clumping around in these rooms alone but, outside, thousands of brightly-clad skiers are milling all over the mountain, or around the laden racks, either parking or extricating their skis, or in the ski school, where tots of four mingle nonchalantly with the cautious forties on the learners' slopes, or clinging to rods on one or another of the conveyor belts properly known as Poma lifts, mounting slowly high above the snow, comfortably seated on the mile-long chairlift; or whizzing down from the tops through winding gullies over gentle bumps and around occasional outcrops of rock to the bottom again.

The art of sitting down swiftly *and* gracefully in a moving chairlift is one that neither James nor I have had much opportunity to learn. On the only occasion we've been right to the summit of the mountain James lost his cap in the process and I tore an embarrassing rent in the seat of my slacks. On the last lap from the lift terminus—it doesn't go quite to the top—I could only hope that the person behind me was also forced to bend almost double as we slogged up the Coronet itself in slippery frozen snow.

(For about half an hour at mid-morning and mid-afternoon during the season non-skiers could then use the chairlift. They were not very popular with the long queues waiting to go up for more thrilling purposes than to see what's to be seen from the top, and this service is now restricted to the off-seasons.)

We had chosen our day well. Under a cloudless sky of baby blue and with scarcely a breath of the icy wind that often assails one on the tops, the Alps lay in a long white arc to west and north, and from the profusion of peaks making from this height (1642 kilometres) an almost uniform wall, one could pick out plainly the slightly more prominent ones: Earnslaw, Aspiring, and, like a small white cloud on the farthest horizon, the monarch of them all, Mt Cook (3765 metres) known to the Maori as Aorangi, the Cloud Piercer.

A grand sight—and one which you'll still see in summer, since the alpine peaks are under perpetual snow—but ears and feet could take no more punishment that winter day; it was not

"A handsome restaurant on two levels." Never did a drink taste better! *National Publicity Studios*

long before we were on our way down again in one one of the lift's 120 double chairs.

Grounded again, we trudged cautiously over the packed snow to watch the Poma lifts in action in Happy Valley and Rocky Gully.

These stand-up lifts work on a somewhat simpler mechanism. With an upright metal shaft between the skier's legs, to which he also holds with his gloved hands, he is "skied" upwards to the desired level before unhooking himself for more independent action. These lifts may be used by anyone but, being removed from the main centre, are particularly in demand for cross-country runs and racing. For those wishing to test their style and speed against experts, races may be arranged with one or another of the thirty instructors, mostly from overseas, whom the company employs.

An organised event of this nature, between professionals and amateurs and known as the Queenstown Pro-Am, was recently instituted by the New Zealand Ski Association and sponsored by Mount Cook Airlines. It is held annually during the same weekend as the already well-established Coronet Cup meeting.

The most extensive developments at the Peak took place in the mid 1960s, when Mr Wigley's programme became so ambitious as to necessitate the forming of a public company. Nor has the end of the road yet been reached: there are immediate plans to install a three-seater chairlift on Greengate Ridges; and because so many thousands more are coming here each successive winter to ski, longterm plans to expand beyond Coronet Peak into a second snowfield are at present afoot. The company's tentative choice at the moment is a basin 1830 metres up on the Remarkable Mountains.

To the uninitiated this seems a remarkable choice—until one remembers the remarkable success that has attended the first ski venture.

Nor have the sister companies lagged behind in this phenomenal development. Subsidiaries of the Mount Cook & Southern Lakes Company now operate landlines throughout both the South and North Islands, and a network of scheduled and feeder airlines served by thirty-three aircraft, from Stewart Island to Waitangi. A special direct service also connects the two main tourist centres, Queenstown in the south with Rotorua in the north.

By motorcoach, by airliner, and by chairlift, the Mount Cook & Southern Lakes company is constantly expanding the transport service which Rodolph Wigley began almost sixty years ago, when he put the first car on the road to Mount Cook.

Coronet chalets. More lifts are planned – and an entirely new site, 1830 metres up on the Remarkables.
National Publicity Studios

Riding the Moonlight trail. "The track is mostly so narrow that they must ride in single file."
National Publicity Studios

11

MOONLIGHT VALLEY

IT'S UNDOUBTED ROMANCE has nothing to do with the traditional moonlight and roses. This high river valley into which you may go either by Land Rover or on horseback was named after Tom Moonlight, who discovered gold in this tributary of the Shotover soon after the initial find at Arthurs Point. The books say he was George, but I stick to Tom because John Seffer, who was born in the valley and lived there all his life, told me that Tom was his name. In any case it's the Moonlight that matters.

There are two routes into the valley, leading off from Queenstown in quite different directions. The trail sets out from Arthurs Point, whereas the Land Rover makes west round Lake

"Lack of experience is no deterrent at all", as this young lady demonstrates. *National Publicity Studios*

Wakatipu for about 10 kilometres, then turns inland on a lonely road to Moke Lake. From there a private road following the Moke tributary for much of the way takes passengers to The Lodge at the head of the Moonlight Valley. In this case it can't be said that either the journey or its end is the better; both are delightful.

Those who prefer to take the trail ride need not necessarily be intending to stay at The Lodge. You may take a half-day ride merely for the fun of it and to see something of the Shotover-Moonlight area; or a full day, in which case you have a picnic lunch on the banks of the Moke; or you may ride up to The Lodge, stay overnight—longer if you care to—and return the next day. If time permits and the weather is right, I think you'd find the last alternative the most rewarding. . . . Oh no, lack of riding experience is really no deterrent at all.

On the Queenstown side of the Arthurs Point bridge there's a very formidable-looking gate leading into a private road. The driver of the Moonlight Stables bus which has brought you the 6.5 kilometres through the gorge ignores the discouraging notice, for this is the road—short but steeply winding—to the company's stables. The river above which they stand at a commanding height is the Shotover.

That the manager is not at the stables this morning is disappointing. I wanted you to meet Mr Murdoch; he's quite a person. But already his men are saddling up and sorting out the riders according to their riding skill or lack of it. Even for those who've never been in the saddle before there's little matter for concern; the horses are all quiet and have been on the trail a hundred times before. Nor will there be any head-on traffic, for the track is mostly so narrow they must ride in single file.

And ride it is, almost all the way, up down and around high above the river. Great heat reflects from these rocky bluffs, and the horses jog lazily along, surefooted through familiarity though the going is rough. While it's possible to

Miner's cabin, Moonlight Gorge. *Alexander Turnbull Library*

valley. There's a bad stretch of shingle-slide to be negotiated, and this is why the horses must now go above it, adding a few miles to the total distance and fording the Moke well upstream of its junction with the Moonlight.

The riders come within sighting distance of the little that remains of the old Moke settlement—a small school and a single cottage—before descending steeply to a grassy clearing by the river, where the hardier have a dip in a clear pool on the lee side of a jutting rock before settling to the hearty consumption of picnic tea and sandwiches. Thereafter full-day riders turn back on their tracks, whilst those whose objective is The Lodge ford the river and turn north into the Moonlight Valley.

We ourselves used to cross into the valley from the lower track at the turbulent junction of the Moke and Moonlight, as did the miners before us, on one of those precarious chairs worked by a pulley-rope.

But that was before Roy Murdoch had his bright idea of instituting a horsetrail.

Roy is a man of many parts: something of a

Beautiful riding country — especially when, as in this picture, the trees are in the golden livery of autumn.
National Publicity Studios

imagine the early diggers coming this same way, each burdened with little more than his blanket, shovel and dish, it seems incredible that later, when the "easy" gold was gone, all the machinery required for the more complicated processes of recovering it from the deeper gravels had to be brought in on packhorses, because some of the steeper bluffs could only be sidled round as it were on a tightrope.

At a point where the riders halt to observe far below the confluence of Moonlight with the larger river, those who've come for only the half-day trip turn back.

The full-day cavalcade, now following the Moonlight, come shortly after this point to a parting of ways. Without hesitation the horses take the higher track, and thereafter the way is more open. But the diggers' track used to continue following the river, and this lower one was the track we invariably took on the several occasions of our walking *en famille* into the

Moke Lake. *National Publicity Studios*

heartbreaker—all the girls fall for him, but unfortunately for them he already has a charming wife; a pleasant manner—though he'll stand for no nonsense; quick, clever hands—he'll mend anything on wheels; boundless knowhow about horses—until quite recently he did all his own breaking-in, shoeing and vetting; terrific drive and enterprise, and a mind astonishingly fertile in Big Ideas.

The stables were only the nucleus. The next accretion was a farm on which to graze and grow feed for the horses, now counted by the score. Then there was the rodeo, whose necessarily impregnable enclosures he built largely himself. Some financial assistance being required when it came to taking over a run of many thousand acres, Roy took that jump by forming a small private company.

It wasn't primarily to run sheep on the hills and cattle in the valleys that they bought the Ben Lomond run, but in order to implement the biggest of Roy's big ideas.

In an astonishingly short time, for he seems to have the knack of inspiring others to work as hard as he does himself, his favourite brainchild was established: on a high plateau in the Moonlight Valley, miles and more miles from a single habitation, he built The Lodge for those who want to opt out of the race for a while, or simply for those who love the back country.

Besides the charm of isolation the buildings themselves have an attractive appearance: timber walls, high-pitched roofs, heavy beams that really do the work beams were meant to do, huge stone fireplace burning beech logs from the nearby forest. And through whatever window you look there are breathtaking views.

Should you not happen to be in convivial mood you can retire to your own small house of two midget bedrooms and a sittingroom, each removed perhaps 20 metres from the others and in a secluded area of its own. My particular favourite overlooks the river and has three ancient beeches at its door.

The company has its own generating plant, but the supply of electricity is not inexhaustible, so the cooking is done on an immense oil-fuelled stove. Meals are *table d'hote* without any continental frills, well cooked and attractively served.

But you may wonder what one *does* in so remote a spot? Well, if absorbing the wonderful air isn't sufficient, there are certainly no fun parks or nightclubs for your entertainment. Nor is there any shooting, so you may as well leave your rifle at home. Not that there isn't anything to shoot, but the deer and goats you will frequently see are for that purpose only. Birds too abound in the beech forest that grows thickly about the river. There are trout in a nearby stream, even traces of gold, and the necessary gear for both fishing and panning is supplied for the asking.

Horses other than these we're riding into the valley are kept permanently at The Lodge for your pleasure. And there are many interesting places to which your own feet will take you.

I should think there's really no reason why you shouldn't do a two-day tramp to Lake Luna and back, if you don't mind rough going and if the river is low. We once walked there ourselves, leaving from Arthurs Point and circling back by way of the Twenty-Mile and Lake Wakatipu. It took us a gruelling but glorious three days, trudging up this wide valley of the Moonlight to where the river turns west under the foothills of Mt Gilbert, finding a track of sorts in the mossy green forest, edging round spurs plunging down to the river, or picking a precarious way in its icy bed.

At several totally impassable bluffs where the miners had cut small access tunnels through the shaly rock we had to bend double, hearts in mouths lest the packs on our backs should touch off disaster. I imagine that crawling through a drainpipe would be much the same experience.

We slept both nights out of doors. The One Ton hut was too decrepit, and at Lake Luna the shepherds' hut was infested with fleas. Why "One Ton" I've never been able to discover. Perhaps some story about a barrel of beer was responsible for the odd name of this very odd old miner's hut? Son One shot a deer, and we lived largely on half-cooked venison, being either too hungry or in too much of a hurry to give it that long slow cooking required for wild game.

From Lake Luna you would now return to The Lodge, but our way in those days continued inexorably on, over a 1220 metre pass—there's a lower one but unfortunately we missed it—and through some miles of untracked country beyond, to the Mount Creighton wharf, where we'd arranged for the steamer to pick us up on her way back from the head of the lake.

All this back country is not quite as inaccessible as it may sound, especially since the Moonlight Company's road was built into The Lodge. Although new and still rather brash in the upper

Moonlight Stables guests on an open trail.
Moonlight Stables Collection

sections, this road over which the Land Rovers bring guests for The Lodge together with all supplies and luggage—including that of the riders—takes a most fascinating route. For about half the distance it follows the Moke Stream from its source in the lake of that name, fording its sparkling waters more than a score of times. And when eventually you turn up the Moonlight Valley, climbing terrace after terrace before actually meeting up with the river itself, there's much of interest to be seen—and heard of. If Roy himself is driving he'll show you some of the more renowned diggings, the largest of which is not far from Moonlight township, of which

nothing now remains but a hut and some alien trees. The occupation of those few of its inhabitants who remained after the easy gold was gone is marked by an enormous crater, where hydrants for raising water and hydraulic nozzles used for sluicing away the hills to get at the richer wash-dirt, lie rusted and half-buried in the gravel floor.

There's a sadness about this ravaged place; it's a relief to drive on, up into the still higher country, where perhaps a grazing stag raises sudden antlers at this fresh intrusion, where "the air's like wine", and where a friendly welcome awaits you at Moonlight Lodge.

Since this book went to press, the Lodge has been temporarily closed.

Queenstown in August, seen from the Skyline Chalet. The Alps "make a long white arc to west and north... a profusion of peaks". *National Publicity Studios*

Ben Lomond: "Reasonably easy
going" if you fancy tackling a
5000-foot climb. *G.A. McCracken*

Mrs H.D. Ritchie, 1951. This 82-year-old lady had known the
gold-fever days and travelled many miles by bullock-waggon.
Her cat's ancestors, too, probably came to Macetown in the
waggons. *Alexander Turnbull Library*

12

BEN LOMOND

JUST BEYOND the Borough camping ground above the wharf you find the notice: "Ben Lomond Walking Track". To climb this mountain under which the town is snugly harboured has always been considered obligatory by residents and visitors alike. The less vigorous will draw the line at a pre-dawn start to see the sunrise, but in any case it's wise to set out early to avoid the heat at just that time you're beginning to flag near the top.

Te Taumata o Hakitekura: behind the Maori name for the mountain there's as usual a story. Hakitekura was born many generations ago at the village of Tahuna. Being of a solitary disposition, or perhaps just rather aloof because she was the daughter of the chief, she would often withdraw from her companions and climb alone to what became known as the Eyrie of Hakitekura. From there she would watch the others swimming in the bay far below; but because the lake itself was so deep and cold none dared swim to the other side.

This feat Hakitekura decided to attempt herself. So taking a firestick wrapped in *raupo* (reed) fibre to keep it dry, she set off one night when all were asleep and, guided by the white-capped peaks across the lake, eventually triumphed in her undertaking. Landing at a point beneath that one of the two mountains nearer to the bay, she then lit an *ahi* (fire), perhaps to warm her frozen limbs, perhaps as a signal to her father to send a *waka* (canoe) to fetch her. So the peaks that had pointed the way were ever after called Ka Kamo o Hakitekura, the Glimmers of Hakitekura, and the landing spot—where the rocks remain blackened to this day—Te Ahi o Hakitekura.

More euphonious names than Cecil and Walter? Even than Refuge Point? As for Ben Lomond—well, it's a pity the Scots shepherd who first climbed it was seized with a fit of nostalgia that day.

The beginning of a climb seems to me always the most arduous. When you get your second wind you'll find this 1520 metre ascent reasonably easy going. Quite open too, with only here and there a group of beeches, affording grateful shade when you pause for a breather.

But it would seem we're to have it cool all the way this morning, though the sun must be well up by now. Unfortunate; if these mountain mists weren't weaving around like a banshee host we'd have much the same outlook from the saddle as Hakitekura had from her eyrie. But no matter; with the exception that from this vantage not a single habitation appears, you've already seen this same tremendous view from the Skyline Chalet.

From the saddle there's a choice of climbs. A clearly-defined track to the left ascends, sharply now, to the top of Ben Lomond, or you could find your own way up the less craggy Bowen Peak, on which there are some interesting underground caves.

A burst of sunshine. And now the mists have massed into the valley below, looking like nothing so much as a vast sea of breakers, suddenly congealed.

Beneath that ocean of foam is the Moke Valley. I once went into it this way, over the saddle and down the other side. Although miners on foot used it as an alternative to the Arthurs Point route, there was no sign of a track when I followed in their wake—a hundred years later. Plenty of time in hand and a built-in objection to retracing my steps dictated the extra miles. Unless I broke a leg on the way down I couldn't fail to find the Moke River at the foot of the pass, and thereafter the familiar track would take me back to Queenstown via Arthurs Point.

When at length I almost bumped into the cottage I'd seen from a spur—literally bumped, for when ankles protested on the steeper pinches I simply rolled or slid on my seat down the tussock slopes—I was more than a little worn. But I knew there'd be the makings of a cup of tea on the hob; although something of an eccentric, the owner was the soul of hospitality.

We had often called before at this lonely cottage, when coming into the Moke or the

Matthew Seffer (*left*) and brother John, who, for all his life was "wedded to the hills and valleys of his youth".
Lakes District Museum

Moonlight from Arthurs Point. Knowing something of our host's habits we always hastily produced our own cups—"The same we used for our picnic lunch, Mr Seffer; it will save you the trouble." But on this occasion I had no cup. What I did have was an outsize thirst, so I shut my eyes when the old man wiped out a cup with old newspaper before pouring the tea.

"You take milk and sugar?"

"Neither, thank you." Better none at all than condensed milk from a tin, or goat's milk from one of his nannies in the yard.

There were goats everywhere, even in the kitchen. They, or their cousins on the hills, were the source of much trouble between John Seffer and those hunters who occasionally found their way into the valley. At the sound of a shot he would rush out after the intruder, shouting and shaking his fists. He had a gun himself, though after a court case in which the prosecutor's hat, neatly punctured with a bullet hole, was produced in evidence, he relied mainly on his tongue to scare off the property any would-be murderer of his beloved goats.

The few acres he called his own were his, I think, more by grace than by right. They're part of the Ben Lomond run, though in his father's time when both Moke and Moonlight were thriving townships, some sections may have been

freehold, then later reincluded in the Crown lands. But whether freed, leased or lent, Mr Seffer certainly had grazing for his horse and land for a vegetable garden close to the house.

It is the last surviving house of many, though the school that served both communities also still stands, a little further downhill. They are the two small buildings that the trail riders glimpse while descending to the riverbed.

Once a week John Seffer used to ride his ancient horse the 14.5 kilometres to Queenstown for supplies, which always included books and newspapers. Although his formal education had necessarily been limited in that isolated spot, he was an inveterate reader—and talker, too, when the opportunity presented itself.

He hadn't far to go for additional reading material, for in one of the row of rooms opening on to the goat yard, a considerable miners' library had been housed since the final exodus more than half a century before. Its quality in both matter and appearance was surprising, until one reflected that the mining community was composed of men and women from many walks of life.

In that small cottage above the Moke John Seffer, three sisters and an older brother had been born. Their mother was an Irishwoman, their father a Russian, Vasilio Sefferovitch. He'd been an army officer and had fought at the Crimea before being lured to New Zealand by

Where have all the children gone? Moke Creek School.
Alexander Turnbull Library

the same tidings of gold that brought so many over the seas in the early 1860s. When it became apparent that he was not to be one of the lucky ones he prudently opened a store in the Moonlight township, but continued to live in the cottage with his family, fossicking again though with little more success, when both settlements had finally died. In these sunny highlands he grew the making of his own wine and tobacco.

The older son, Matthew, had better luck than his father. John once showed me where his claim had been on the Moonlight. He died shortly before we came to Queenstown, and the Misses Seffer then went to live in the village. But not John; he was married to the hills and valleys of his youth.

John had been much attached to his brother Matthew and, upon the occasion of my descending on him from the pass, we were talking about Matthew when the old man went into an adjoining room and returned carrying a rather soiled white handkerchief with care. Upon his opening it on the table, there to my astonished gaze lay a fist-sized pile of nuggets, most of them about the size of a thumbnail.

Trying not to look at his patched clothes, thinking of the cracked dishes and the ancient black stove, I exclaimed, "But these are worth hundreds!"

To which he replied: "They've a value to me far above money; they were Matthew's, you see."

Pensive thoughts apparently following one on the other, Mr Seffer then took a key from a nail behind the door, and showed me into a room whose existence I hadn't even suspected before.

"Here it's been, just like you see it now, through all the years since my father carried my mother a bride into this house over ninety years ago."

The room was perfectly clean and neat, furnished in the Victorian manner with shiny black horsehair, balloon-backs, rag rugs, kerosene lamps, a whatnot, and a little mill that had ground the family coffee "through the years".

John was the last of the family to survive. I prefer not to think of him in his later years, when he became extremely cantankerous and the

All that is left of a miner's house and dam, Billy Creek. Was there fortune here — or failure? Only the great tree could tell you. *National Publicity Studios*

chip on his shoulder assumed the proportions of a log. I like to think of him pottering in his garden or in the old sluicing claim below the cottage, petting his goats, or walking his nag round what is now the riding trail, those nine miles to Queenstown.

No, don't be alarmed; neither have I any thought of adding those extra miles to this expedition. Once was enough, and this last steep pinch up the mountain tells me my breathing apparatus isn't what it used to be.

There, we've made it. And if you've a mind to, you can scratch your name on the cairn. . . . Yes, it's been worth it. Just to have this marvellous feeling of—accomplishment? Omnipotence? Release? Just to see, beyond that seeming limitless field of ranges stretching in great furrows east, west and north, the faint white peaks of the Alps, with Aorangi, Cloud in the Sky, queening it among the lesser multitude.

"Range upon range." The highest peak on the horizon is that of Mt Earnslaw. *National Publicity Studios*

Looking up the lake towards Mt Alfred and the Forbes mountain beyond with Mount Creighton station, base for fishing and deerstalking safaris on the promontory in the middle of the photograph. *National Publicity Studios*

13

PARADISE

ALTHOUGH AN H & H COACH runs on occasion beyond its normal terminus at Glenorchy to Paradise, it stays so briefly in this lovely spot that it's more satisfying, we think, to drive your car or to hire one for the purpose. There's enough scenic grandeur both en route and upon arrival to keep you happy all day. So pop the picnic basket in the boot and away we go.

And go-slow should be the driver's policy at least as far as the head of the lake. It's a one-way road, as yet unsealed, and with only at intervals a widened passing bay. There's hardly a chain that doesn't twist, turn and switchback, often high above the lake and close to its edge where some particularly bold bluff allows no more than a grudging passage. But with reasonable care it's not a dangerous road and the surface is passably good.

A little beyond the Five-Mile the Moke road branches inland, but ours continues, following closely the shoreline of the lake until it presently takes a major bend into the north reach. Up and up it climbs, and it's now that you must watch for what is surely the eighth wonder of the world.

The full beauty of it doesn't burst upon you until the car round Bennetts Bluff; from here the green rolling foreground completes the stupendous panorama which, with a catch to the breath, you've already glimpsed a few miles back. There, heaping across the wide headlands of the lake, lie range upon range studded with peaks high-crowned with everlasting snows. But adequately to describe it is impossible; you must see for yourself this glory which, once seen, you'll carry in mind for always without the feeble help of words.

The names of these mountains too, are a joy. There's the classic names like Erebus, Somnus—that's the second on the far left, shaped like a church—Momus, Nox, Chaos and Cosmus, Pluto and Cerberus; the seven perky peaks named somewhat tritely the Seven Brides; and Earnslaw, monarch of them all at something over 2740 metres.

In the middle foreground is forested Mt Alfred—the only one not perpetually topped with snow—firmly dividing the Rees and Dart Valleys.

But we must press on. Though you may feel that you're already there, it's quite some distance yet to Paradise.

Truth must out: the romantic name has a prosaic origin. It's said to have been so called because the first man to push a way into this wide flat in the upper valley of the Dart found it teeming with paradise duck. I myself prefer to think he was indulging in a play upon words. Of all our highcountry valleys this is surely the most serene, the most beautiful, the most fertile.

After leaving the lake at Glenorchy you drive for several miles through open farmlands in the lower Rees Valley before crossing the bridge into the Dart. A further few miles through enchanting beech forest brings you then to your goal.

Again I deplore the poverty of words. When I say that the valley is wide, far-reaching, very green, ringed on two sides by beech forest, on a third by the Dart River and the fourth by Diamond Lake, and that the distant mountains you saw from Bennetts Bluff form its intimate background, the printed words convey nothing of the feeling-tone, the atmostphere, the whatever-it-is that lifts the spirit here. Space, quiet, solitude. . . .

Not that it's entirely uninhabited. Apart from free-ranging herds of Hereford cattle as thick as sheep on a Southland farm, two families live in the valley. It is in fact quite an old settlement—as you'll be led to suspect by the architectural style of Arcadia, the homestead overlooking Diamond Lake.

Arcadia is what, as children, we used to call a storybook house, all gables and turrets and balconies. And the little that has survived of all the human dramas that must have been played through the years within its walls, is itself such stuff as tales are made of. It was built by a Mr Fenn, a young Englishman who bought the run

Paradise duck, native to New Zealand and abundant in the high country. The female's plumage is showier than that of the sombre male. *National Publicity Studios*

then known as Paradise Flats, after the Government had subdivided Gilbert Rees's enormous holding into several such smaller runs. Shortly afterwards, Fenn sold a small freehold area in the south-west corner of the valley to the internationally-known architect William Mason, who built there as a retreat a small stone dwelling that was the nucleus of the present Paradise House.

Much enlarged, Paradise House became a boarding establishment in 1887. The Mr and Mrs Aitken who'd bought it for the purpose had an attractive daughter whom Fenn the runholder wished to marry. The parents, however, were against the match, possibly because the suitor was a "remittance man". The stigma then attaching to the phrase appears in this case to have had little justification. Indeed he had qualifications, over and beyond the fact that he received regular allowances from his family in England, that might have commended him to most. Formerly a Cambridge rowing blue and the all-England sculling champion of his day, he must have won further acclaim in the colony of his choice by importing a prize strain of sheep and establishing a successful stud in the Valley.

But whatever the reason, Fenn had no success in winning the wife of his choice, and in a fit of pique or smouldering resentment he finally built

Arcadia, installed a manager, and ran it as a rival guesthouse in the remote and beautiful spot that had quickly become renowned amongst discerning travellers, particularly artists from overseas.

The experiment lasted for only about a decade, after which Arcadia changed hands and became a private dwelling. But Paradise House continued to flourish under the same proprietorship for more than half a century, during which the Aitken family were known far and wide for their worth and hospitality.

So, for that matter, were their successors, the Veints, though by their time the new high-pressure tourism was beginning to pass this quiet valley by. Mrs Veint was an excellent cook—as we had occasion to learn while staying there when our family was young. Jim Veint, who now owns Arcadia station in partnership with his father, was then just a small boy, matching our own youngest son in devilry. His father, Lloyd Veint, was a renowned back-country man, deerstalker, mountaineer, horseman. He used to take us across the swift-flowing Dart on horseback to the Route Burn, or up the Rees Valley towards Mt Earnslaw and Lochnagar. The Veint parents now live in Arcadia, the son and his young family in a new house a little removed from the old homestead.

Paradise House is still occupied, though no longer a guesthouse. Mr Miller, who bought it from the Veints, has unfortunately since died, but the entire family were there—parents, son and daughter—when James and I first met them some years ago on one of our periodical returns to the siren valley. The reason for leaving their home in Bermuda to settle in this remote corner of the world was to save the life of their only son David, who suffered from a severe form of asthma. Having tried fruitlessly every treatment recommended by a succession of doctors in many parts of the USA, the parents finally grasped at what proved to be no straw. Mr Miller told us the story.

"I know of only one place, this last doctor told us, where David might be able to live. It's a small place called Queenstown in a small country in the Pacific called New Zealand. Dry alpine air all the year round."

"And so," Mrs Miller added, "we simply packed up and came—here, when we found that Paradise was for sale."

There was no need to ask if the treatment had been effective. David, now a young man, was blooming with health and enthusiasm.

Although Arcadia owns the greater part of the valley, Paradise has something over 80 hectares on the western side. It carries a few cattle, but most of the property is heavily bushed. Through a large area of this mainly beech forest we tramped with David that day. His joy in it, his pride in it, labelled him already a true New Zealander.

He has other interests too. His science degree, for which he qualified by correspondence with considerable help from his parents, has been put to practical use on the home front. They installed their own hydro-electric plant, also an ingenious mechanism which ensures an unfailing water supply from the upper reaches of a small bush stream. And now that David is himself a family man with two young children, a more ambitious project has recently got under way with the construction of a small sawmill in a well-screened clearing behind the house. Here David plans to dress his own felled timbers for the replacement

Diamond Lake holds both brown and rainbow trout. In the background are the Humboldt Mountains.
National Publicity Studios

Paradise House opened as a guest-house in 1887, and this coachload of early tourists is on its way there.
Radcliffe Collection, Alexander Turnbull Library

of the aged and rambling Paradise House with an alpine-style home that will be worthy of its magnificent setting.

The stream that provides their domestic water supply also serves the half-dozen huts and cottages, each in its own private clearing, that are another of the Miller inovations. One or two are newly built, but most were abandoned cottages bought in various parts of the district. These they transported to the valley, renovated, and furnished as holiday houses for people who, like themselves, prefer the quiet of the country to the clamour of the modern tourist resort.

For the active, however, there's plenty to do: here are Virginian deer on Mt Alfred, brown and rainbow trout in Diamond Lake, and the upper Dart is a fascinating river to explore. If you're in luck, as James and I were during a happy week-end spent in one of the cottages, David may take you to the Rock Burn in his jeep, up past Sylvan Lake, across the Dart, then on foot into the primeval forest, with the merry little tributary careering through it in leaps and rushes. Now you are in the very heart of the classic mountains, Nox and Niobe feeding in from the north, Somnus and Momus from the south.

Upon another occasion of our staying in Paradise, James and I made a memorable climb to the glacier on the West Peak of Earnslaw. . . . but enough of past pleasures. Let's open the picnic basket and settle for present ones. Here, on the leaf-brown earth beneath this enormous beech tree. Look, there's a flock of small green parakeets. . . . This knowing little bush robin with his head on one side, sizing us up or looking for crumbs—*ssh!* See that? He settled for a moment right on my finger.

And that? That was a bellbird "singing in the wilderness". No book of verse, no flask of wine—only thermos coffee. Yet surely this is "Paradise enow"?

Routeburn country, with the Somnus Range beyond. *Alexander Turnbull Library*

Speed, scenery, safety. *Kingston Cruiser* ferries visitors between Kingston and Queenstown, 50 at a time.
NZ Railways

Kingston Flyer, "beautifully restored", winds her way through summer pastures.

14

EXIT SOUTH

SUPPOSING THE VISITOR means to go farther south upon leaving Queenstown, there's a more unusual way of doing so than either driving or flying. It's not of course obligatory to exit in this manner, but it's certainly more fun. Alternatively, while still in Queenstown you may take this trip there and back in the one day. "There" could be only as far as the foot of the lake in the *Kingston Cruiser;* or it could be to Lumsden, about 64 kilometres further on, by transferring to the *Kingston Flyer.*

The launch and the steam train connect three times a day during the summer season, bringing passengers to and from Lumsden, a central junction for the main Otago and Southland towns and tourist resorts. The full return trip, however, can be fitted in only once a day, and for this you must be ready to set out from the jetty—the one immediately east of the main wharf—at 8.45 am.

The *Kingston Cruiser* is a newcomer to the lake and, unlike the *Flyer,* which belongs to the Railways Department, is privately owned and operated. Indeed Mr Rolfe is not only both owner and skipper; he also built the handsome fifty-passenger cabin cruiser himself. In such capable hands one feels it hardly necessary even to wear a lifejacket, but the weather man is not so dependable, and in the unlikelihood of an emergency they're always on hand.

Once outside the harbour, the *Cruiser* steers a southerly course past the familiar Cecil Peak towards Halfway Bay station—at whose wharf, you may recall, the *Earnslaw* landed Mr Lucas's tourist bus a few years ago. And there, leaping out of the lake, are the craggy Bayonet Peaks behind which he drove it to Cecil Peak. Opposite and behind the homestead are the Rough Peaks of the Eyre Mountains.

Halfway Bay is in a snug position on wide flats at the mouth of the Lochy—an excellent flyfishing river but accessible only from the lake or from a droving road at the back of the run. As we pass, the sun-drenched homestead appears very peaceful in its setting of trees with the waters of the lake gently lapping its foreshore.

But in winter, when only the rocky ribs of the encompassing mountains can be seen thrusting darkly through the snow, it would seem a less desirable spot to live in. Nor is the lake at all times so serenely blue.

A little beyond Halfway Bay on the opposite side where the road to the south goes coiling round the foothills of the Remarkables, the Devil's Staircase rises in giant steps over into the neighbouring valley. Between these two points is the narrowest and deepest part of the lake (390 metres) which in rough weather can carry a dangerous rip. In the *Wakatipians* Alfred Duncan tells of a mishap that occurred here, and of a rescue which for sheer courage and fortitude would be hard to equal.

The hero of the incident was Jack Taewa, more commonly known as Maori Jack, an employee at the Rees station in Queenstown Bay. (Incidentally, it was he who showed the first prospector on the Arrow where to find gold, the soft metal on which the Maori set no store at all.) On a voyage south from the Rees homestead Maori Jack, Mitchell, an English cadet, and Rodgers, a down-country runholder, were capsized when in full sail during a sudden winter storm. The two Europeans clung to the keel until their hands were too numb to hold on, but Jack—who could easily have swum ashore—kept hauling each one back as he lost his grip and began to sink. Eventually while Maori Jack was rescuing Mitchell, Rodgers entirely disappeared.

Jack then swam to the opposite side and held Mitchell's hands in his own across the inverted boat, meanwhile "chanting a Maori death song". Suddenly he stopped singing, shouted a question, then leaning far over the keel drew a claspknife from Mitchell's waistcoat pocket with his teeth. Leaving him a moment he dived under the boat, cut the halyards, pulled the mast out of its socket, rose to the surface and was now able to turn the boat over and scramble in, dragging Mitchell after him.

Although the boat was half full of water, he managed to paddle it to shore at Halfway Bay—

Halfway Bay homestead in the very early days. But there was no dwelling here when Maori Jack rescued the drowning man.
Hocken Library

where of course there was then no habitation—and to carry the now unconscious Mitchell to higher ground. When the other had revived a little Jack set off for help to von Tunzelmann's station and, incredible as it must seem to those familiar with this ruggard and trackless country, he reached Mount Nicholas before daybreak that same night. Then, still undefeated, he crossed by boat with von Tunzelmann to the Rees homestead.

The end of the story is almost as fantastic as the rest. When Rees and his men found Mitchell later that day, a collie dog was seen to run off into the scrub. But for the fact that shortly after Jack had left him the previous evening, this animal had appeared from nowhere and lain on his body all night and most of next day, Mitchell was certain he could not have survived the cold. There was apparently no mystery about the identity of the dog; as a pup it had escaped from a boat near Halfway Bay and had managed to survive as a wild dog.

It is pleasing to record that when Mitchell eventually recovered from his ordeal, he gave Jack "a handsome silver hunting watch" engraved with appropriate words of gratitude. Admiring friends contributed to a subscription that provided Jack with a waggon and team of bullocks, with which he made a small fortune on the diggings; and finally, he was awarded the British Humane Society's medal for gallantry.

It's perhaps as well for your peace of mind that it's no longer necessary to go through the gut under sail.

Although new, the *Cruiser* has re-established quite an old service. When first we began coming to Wakatipu we used to travel by express train, the *Kingston Flyer*, to the foot of the lake, and from there by *Earnslaw* to Queenstown. As the lake road was gradually improved the time came when the steamer service was discontinued, and shortly after the two-lane paved highway was opened in 1962, the rail service also was superseded, except for freight, by that of the road.

Some two or three years ago, however, when NZ Railways had converted from coal to oil, the Government decided to retain two of its old steam trains. One of these is the *Kingston Flyer*—to which, unless you mean to return immediately on the *Cruiser* with the new complement of passengers embarking for Queenstown, you now transfer.

The name of the *Flyer* is as old as the train—though the latter looks far from decrepit. The locomotive and the cars have been beautifully restored. The white plume of smoke, Lincoln green paint and polished brass of the *Kingston Flyer* have become once again a familiar and a handsome sight.

For the passengers' comfort and choice there's a refreshment car, fully licensed, two ordinary first-class cars and one of those we used to call a birdcage, all with the original fittings except that the seats have been cushioned with plushy foam rubber.

For 10 kilometres south of Kingston the railway runs through a terminal moraine, relic of the last Ice Age when, from ten to fifteen million years ago, increasing warmth gradually melted the immense glacier that filled the Wakatipu basin. The whole wide area between the Hector Range and the Eyre Mountains is littered with boulders, and the sparse vegetation appears to subsist on nothing but gravel.

Winding through this lumber is a former riverbed, now filled with flax and *toetoe* (pampas grass), but obviously once a major outlet to the lake. It is thought that a tributary of the Mataura River, which both road and rail now follow for several kilometres to Parawa, has an underground source in the lake.

From Parawa the country appears more fertile, hilly rather than mountainous, though there's an area of wasteland in the wide-spreading riverbeds immediately north of Lumsden.

Lumsden itself, at the head of a prosperous farming valley and an important road and railway junction, ought to be more attractive than it is. But neither its undistinguished appearance nor the reason for it will much concern those passing through. Here are the outgoing buses all lined up beside the railway station, and the majority of passengers from the *Flyer* sort themselves into one or another of those labelled Dunedin, Invercargill, Milford Sound, Manapouri, Te Anau, or Queenstown. Some who have arrived upon these railways buses or in their own cars are transferring themselves and their luggage to the train before joining the crowd in one or other of the only two restaurants, for lunch.

Now the big hand of the post office clock is on one. The bus passengers still have ten minutes to spare, but "All aboard!" shouts the guard, as those choosing this more novel form of transport settle themselves in the comfortable seats of the *Kingston Flyer*.

At the foot of Lake Wakatipu there's another reshuffle. Vintage-train fans will perhaps remain on the *Flyer* for the trip back to Lumsden, whilst others transfer to the bus about to tackle the road round the lake. But most will be boarding the *Kingston Cruiser*, to be taken or returned to Queenstown, top place of their choice in the south.

Three ages of tourist travel: *(far left)* a four-horse brake of the 1890s at Arrowtown, two Rodolph Wigley Darracqs, *circa* 1914; and a Mount Cook HS 748 after flying in from Auckland and Rotorua. *Alexander Turnbull Library and Mount Cook Co.*

ABOUT THIS BOOK

THE PRE-PAKEHA MAORI knew Lake Wakatipu and wove colourful legends around it. European explorers sighted it in the 1850s. Rees and his friend von Tunzelmann settled here in 1860. Gold fever broke out in 1863 and, when it was all over, Queenstown's convalescence was helped along by a Government which realised that the beauty of lake and forest and rivers must be an all-time magnet for visitors.

Their confidence has been fully justified. For over 100 years Queenstown's loveliness has been attracting visitors and residents in ever-increasing numbers. Few holiday resorts anywhere in the world can have so much to offer throughout the twelve months of the year.

Mrs Preston has known the lake and its environs for many years, and was brought up on its legends and the facts of its history. In this book she shares her love and understanding with her readers, guiding them around the town, taking them on excursions across the lake, up and down the rivers, over to Arrowtown, Macetown and Skippers, to Moonlight Valley, Ben Lomond and Paradise, up to Coronet Peak — a born *raconteuse* and a delightfully friendly companion.

It all makes fascinating reading and will add immeasurably to the pleasure of a Queenstown holiday. And, with its wealth of illustrations, what a memento it is of such a holiday!

Florence Preston was born in Invercargill and educated at Southland Girls' High School and at the University of Otago. Her name as a writer was established by her novels —*A Gallows Tree*, *Harvest of Daring*, *Great Refusals*, and *The Gay Pretensions* — and, as the present book clearly demonstrates, her factual work is equally impressive. She and her husband have three sons and one daughter, all of whom the reader will meet in this book, and have their home just outside Queenstown.

OTHER REED BOOKS

QUEENSTOWN
by Peter Beadle

New Zealand's most popular tourist resort and its surrounding districts are brilliantly recorded by the pen and brush of Peter Beadle. The perfect gift or holiday souvenir.

POPEYE LUCAS: QUEENSTOWN
by F.J. Lucas

The life story of an independent, engaging character, Fred Lucas, who founded Southern Scenic Airways (Queenstown) and pioneered tourist and agricultural aviation. As many as 14,000 visitors a year enjoy his personally conducted tours of Cecil Peak Station.

THE ROAD TO SKIPPERS
by Danny A. Knudson

This book will help give a greater appreciation of the awe-inspiring landscapes between Queenstown and Skippers, which are surely the most spectacular in New Zealand and it provides a permanent pictorial record of this highly popular tourist journey.